THE
MAYAN
PROPHECIES

THE MAYAN

PROPHECIES

2012

THE MESSAGE AND THE VISION

GERALD BENEDICT

WATKINS PUBLISHING

LONDON

For Rebecca, Ben and David Woolman
"Time is nature's way of keeping everything from happening at once."
(variously attributed)

The Mayan Prophecies
Gerald Benedict

Distributed in the USA and Canada by
Sterling Publishing Co., Inc.
387 Park Avenue South
New York, NY 10016-8810

This edition first published in the UK and USA in 2010 by
Watkins Publishing
Sixth Floor, Castle House
75–76 Wells Street
London W1T 3QH

Managing Editor: Christopher Westhorp
Editorial Assistant: Elinor Brett
Managing Designer: Suzanne Tuhrim
Picture Research: Julia Ruxton
Commissioned artwork: Lasse Skarbovik

Library of Congress Cataloging-in-Publication Data

Benedict, Gerald.
 The Mayan prophecies 2012 : the message and the vision /
Gerald Benedict.
   p. cm.
 Includes index.
 ISBN 978-1-907486-33-3
 1. Maya calendar. 2. Maya astrology. 3. Mayas--Prophecies. 4.
Two thousand twelve, A.D. 5. Twenty-first century--Forecasts. I.
Title.

 F1435.3.C14B46 2010
 133.5089'9742--dc22

                                        2010020393

10 9 8 7 6 5 4 3 2 1

Typeset in DIN
Color reproduction by Colourscan
Printed in Hong Kong by Imago

For information about custom editions, special sales, premium
and corporate purchases, please contact Sterling Special Sales
Department at 800-805-5489 or specialsales@sterlingpub.com.

Notes
Abbreviations used throughout this book:
CE Common Era (the equivalent of AD)
BCE Before the Common Era (the equivalent of BC)

Endpaper illustration
Pages from the *Dresden Codex* with astronomical tables which
describe the cycles of the moon, identified with the goddess of
illness and childbirth.

Page 2 The "wall of skulls" at Chichén Itzá (see also pages
136–137 and page 138).

CONTENTS

FOREWORD

The attention the Maya people have attracted in recent years has been gathering momentum. The main reason for this is that the Mayan Long Count era, which began on 13 August 3114BCE, terminates with the solstice on 21 December 2012. This has generated a great deal of speculation about what will happen on that date or during the years that follow. Astronomically, the solstice marks the completion of the cycle of precession and a phenomenon termed galactic synchronization (see pages 84–87) – an extraordinary cosmic alignment that occurs approximately every 26,000 years. For those of us who are living at the time of this rare event and beyond, there appears to be a Mayan prophecy addressed specifically to us: that we are in some way responsible for finding a solution to the predicted problems and crises (see pages 166–169).

Many books have been written about the significance of 2012 and the prophecies. Some books suggest that the world is about to end, or that the Earth faces some life-threatening catastrophe. Others claim that the Maya acquired their knowledge from extra-terrestrials.

Growing interest in the Maya and their civilization has resulted in "Mayanism" – not the scholarship of historians

and anthropologists, but a collection of miscellaneous interpretations of this historical culture rooted in the notion that the Maya had perceptions of life, the cosmos, nature and ecology that do not fit with Western rationalism. The energy for Mayanism is partly generated by questions about Mayan history and culture that we have not yet been able to answer, such as how they came by their advanced knowledge of mathematics and astronomy. Such unknowns constitute a kind of "mystery" that attracts speculation, in which scholarship is eschewed in favour of a New Age mysticism that desires enlightenment and revelation. The Mayan prophetic tradition encourages this because it appeals most strongly to those who wish to claim esoteric knowledge and special insight for their own world-view.

Contemporary elders of the Maya are saddened and disconcerted by the way that some Westerners have appropriated their teachings, and by the more extreme interpretations of the prophecies, cosmology and eschatology. This book presents a reasoned, balanced account of the calendars and prophecies of Mayan civilization, and its history, culture, religion and mythology.

Gerald Benedict, Payrignac, France

INTRODUCTION:
THE MAYAN WORLD

THE LOST CIVILIZATION

In the late 1830s an American, John Lloyd Stephens, and an Englishman, Frederick Catherwood, exploring in the heart of the tropical rainforests of central Yucatán, came across the most extraordinary abandoned buildings, sculptures and carved upright stones or stelae. The men's interest had been sparked by earlier accounts of ruined Mesoamerican cities in Mexico and Central America from explorers such as Alexander von Humboldt and Juan Galindo, featuring long-overgrown places such as Palenque and Copán.

The first ruins Stephens and Catherwood had encountered were of Mayapan in northwest Yucatán. The pair continued and were to be overwhelmed by the grandeur of what they stumbled across during 1839 and 1840. At Copán in Honduras, Stephens wrote: "We sat down on the very edge of the wall, and strove in vain to penetrate the mystery by which we were surrounded. Who were the people who built this city? . . . America, say historians, was peopled by savages; but savages never reared these structures . . . . We asked Indians who made them, and their dull answer was . . . 'Who knows?'"

The accounts (with engravings based on Catherwood's drawings) of their exploratory travels – *Incidents of Travel in Central America, Chiapas, and Yucatán* (1841) and *Incidents of Travel in Yucatán* (1843) – were best sellers that introduced to the Western world the civilization of the ancient Maya. (A limited-edition colour work was produced by Catherwood in 1844: *Views of Ancient Monuments in Central America, Chiapas, and Yucatán*.)

Many of the places were being written about for the first time and what the two men achieved amounted to the recovery of a "lost civilization", an event that excited the imagination not only of scholars but also of the nineteenth-century public, in much the same way as the novel *Lost Horizon* (1933) by James Hilton was to excite popular belief in the existence of a Himalayan utopia called Shangri-La.

Stephens suggested three areas for further research: surviving manuscripts, decipherment of the hieroglyphs found at the sites, and a search for an actual "lost city" where the Maya might still be living as they originally did, unaware of the outside world. The tragedy of the first suggestion is that only a few texts have survived; the second has been fully realized, opening up the Mayan world for everyone; the third remains a fantasy.

In fact, the third suggestion overlooked the fact that the Maya were not a people consigned to the past. Today, they number around six million, including those who live by the ancient calendars, maintaining the original beliefs and shamanic practices. What Stephens and Catherwood undoubtedly achieved was to grant the Maya a proper place among the great civilizations of humankind and one that remains an enduring object of fascination and study.

THE GOVERNOR'S PALACE at Uxmal, overgrown by jungle vegetation, as it was first encountered by Stephens and Catherwood. This chromo-lithograph was created by Frederick Catherwood for *Views of Ancient Monuments in Central America, Chiapas, and Yucatán*, first published in London in 1844.

THE HOME OF THE MAYA

Mayan civilization developed over a long period in an area that is a diverse mixture of mountains, low marshland, lush tropical rainforest (with specialized flora and fauna) and arid terrain made habitable only through the development of sophisticated irrigation and water-storage systems.

The Maya inhabited three major climatic areas: temperate, tropical and semi-arid. From western El Salvador to the southern mountains of Guatemala, where the Tajumulco volcano (13,845ft/4,220m) is the highest point in Central America, the climate is temperate. In the southern half of the Yucatán peninsula heavy rain supports the rainforests and the climate is tropical. Many of the ancient cities are located there. A large part of this area has been protected since 1990 when a nature reserve larger than Yellowstone National Park was created within the El Petén region of Guatemala, called the Maya Biosphere Reserve. In the northern part of Yucatán the climate is semi-arid: the top soil has been eroded, scrub struggles to survive and a geology of porous limestone means that the rivers and lakes form subterraneously.

Mayan society, highland and lowland, was founded upon farming. In the swampier areas of the Yucatán, Mayan agriculture was based on an innovative raised field system, irrigated by a grid of canals. Meanwhile, in the forests, "slash and burn" techniques were used. However, an area of cleared land was viable only for a few years, and when it was worked out the community had to move on.

The staple crop of the Maya was maize, or corn, a fact that was amply reflected in Mayan mythology and the pantheon of gods. The Maya also cultivated the breadnut tree (*Brosimum alicastrum*, or *ramón* in Spanish) and it is likely that these edible nuts were a "famine food", something to fall back on when maize was in short supply. The creation myth in the *Popul Vuh* describes how, after several failed attempts with a variety of materials (including wood), the gods finally succeeded in creating the first humans out of maize (see page 95). The Maya personified maize as a young lord, often with an elongated, tonsured head. Thereafter, emphasizing the importance of maize to Mayan society, each ruler assumed the form and attributes of a maize god.

Mayan history is conventionally organized into three approximate periods: the Pre-Classic (c.2000BCE–c.250CE), the Classic (c.250–c.900CE) and the Post-Classic (c.900–1521CE). At its height, toward the end of the eighth century CE, efficient Mayan agriculture was supporting a population of approximately eight million people.

THE PRE-CLASSIC PERIOD

The earliest prehistoric settlements in the region date back to c.6000BCE, mostly in locations along the coast

THE MAYAN REALM is mostly highlands and jungle, straddling the modern-day states of Belize, El Salvador, Guatemala, Honduras and Mexico (see inset).

MEXICO

BELIZE

GUATEMALA

HONDURAS

EL SALVADOR

Dzibilchaltun

Mérida

Mayapan

Chichén Itzá

Uxmal

Kabah

Tulúm

Sayil

Jaina Island

Labna

NORTHERN AREA

Hochob

Chicanna

Cerros

Comalcalco

Calakmul

El Mirador

Nakbé

Uaxactun

Holmul

CENTRAL AREA

Buenavista

Palenque

Tikal

Naranjo

Piedras Negras

Belize City

Tayasal

Yaxhá

Yaxchilán

Bonampak

Altar de Sacrificios

Seibal

Nebaj

Quirigua

SOUTHERN AREA

Izapa

Kaminaljuyu

Copán

Guatemala City

where there was ready access to a regular supply of food. By the beginning of the Pre-Classic period, farming villages had been established throughout the central and northern regions subsequently identified with the Maya: these were the precursors of the substantial towns and cities that were to grow up over time, accompanied by the construction of monumental palaces, temples, pyramids and the inscribing of stonework and stelae.

Sites built during this formative era include El Mirador and Nakbé, in the north of the El Petén region of modern-day Guatemala; Tikal, also in El Petén, where between 400 and 300 BCE construction began at what was to become one of the Maya's largest urban sites (see page 64); and Cerros, on the coast of northern Belize, which was an important trading centre in the late Pre-Classic era, with temples, plazas, two ballcourts and a canal system.

THE CLASSIC PERIOD

During the Classic period (c.250–c.900CE) agricultural production became more intensive and the independently ruled Mayan city-states were frequently drawn into conflict with one another. Tikal became powerful and expansionary – and just to the north of it is Uaxactun, whose leaders in 378CE were defeated by a war party from Tikal led by a warrior named Fire is Born, who then forged a combined entity that was to dominate the region for centuries.

Among the lowland Maya stone monuments were erected, inscribed with information such as the Long Count dates (see pages 22–27). The stepped pyramid was a product of the age and the architectural arrangement of sites was intended to provide sightlines for astronomical observation, of which copious records were kept over a long period of time.

THE OLMEC MOTHER CIVILIZATION

The Olmec were a proto-Mesoamerican civilization, flourishing c.1400–c.400BCE, that occupied the region around the southern tip of the Gulf of Mexico, with the modern-day city of San Lorenzo at its centre, and comprising parts of the modern states of Veracruz and Tabasco.

The Olmec period overlaps with the middle and late Pre-Classic Mayan civilization. The Olmec are best known for having carved colossal heads out of basalt, face masks out of jade and for the construction of artificial "mountains", which were to influence

Mayan pyramid architecture. The Olmec also developed a calendric system, a mythology, a shamanic religion and a full-time priesthood. An incised tablet dated 900BCE suggests that they also had Mesoamerica's oldest writing system.

A CAPTIVE SEIZED FOR SACRIFICE can be seen in this scene from a vase. A hunting party of ornately dressed warriors hold a naked and bound man, who will be beheaded in a ritual execution to honour the gods (note the decapitation instrument held aloft by the first warrior behind the prisoner).

Three of the most famous Classic period sites are Copán, Palenque and Chichén Itzá. Copán, in western Honduras, was the site of an important Mayan kingdom that developed between the fifth and the ninth centuries CE. Copán is famed for its portrait stelae and the carved decoration adorning its buildings. The much smaller city-state of Palenque is in the Mexican state of Chiapas. It was at its height in the seventh century, but was abandoned toward the end of the ninth and became overgrown by jungle. Among the city's greatest monuments are those that record its history and the genealogy of its ruling dynasty, the most famous king being Pacal, whose tomb is within the Temple of Inscriptions (see pages 76–83). When the Spanish first arrived in the vicinity of Palenque in the 1520s, the district was only sparsely populated.

The large site of Chichén Itzá, in north-central Yucatán, remained the regional focus of Mayan life and culture into the early Post-Classic period. The site has a variety of architectural styles, including those associated with cultures from central Mexico – this stylistic mix may be a consequence of the migration of people into northern Yucatán, or may be simply the result of cultural diffusion.

THE POST-CLASSIC PERIOD

The abandonment of the major sites at the end of the ninth century and the "disappearance" of the Maya brought the Classic period to an end (see pages 50–55) The Post-Classic period endured until the invasion of the "mountain of foreigners" in the sixteenth century.

Despite the catastrophe in the forests of the south, Mayan life and culture continued strongly in the northern part of the Yucatán peninsula – for example, at Uxmal and Mayapan. Uxmal (meaning "built three times") was founded in 500CE, and major construction continued there until around 1200CE, producing the Governor's Palace, the Pyramid of the Magician, the Nunnery Quadrangle and a ballcourt. Uxmal's ruling Xiu dynasty declined because of the demise of their allies at Chichén Itzá. The regional balance of power then shifted to Mayapan, meaning "banner of the Mayas", and to its ruling family the Cocoom. Mayapan became the cultural and political capital of the Maya in Yucatán until the 1440s. The site holds some 4,000 structures, including the Temple of Kukulcan (the Mayan version of the Aztec Quetzalcoatl). The Cocoom, through intermarriage and with the help of Tabascan mercenaries, ruled for 250 years until they were overcome.

To a greater or lesser extent, all of these societies contributed to Mayan development, influencing mythology, religion, architecture and social organization.

THE COLLAPSE OF MAYAN CIVILIZATION

The dramatic failure of Classic Mayan civilization, from c.800 to c.925 CE, has never been satisfactorily explained. Despite the fact that the Maya had remarkably accurate prophecies relating to their own history (see pages 51–55), no pre-800CE prophecy has survived that foretold the Maya's rapid decline and the abandonment of the great ceremonial sites in the forests.

The widespread reduction in monumental and commemorative activity – buildings, inscriptions, stelae raising and genealogical recording – suggests the "end of history" for these city-states. The collapse began in the

TIMELINE OF MAYAN CIVILIZATION

c.6000BCE PREHISTORIC PERIOD
Human settlements along the coast

c.2600BCE Evidence of humans at Cuello

c.2000BCE–c.250CE PRE-CLASSIC PERIOD

c.1500–c.400BCE Olmec civilization flourishes

c.1400BCE Nakbé founded, central area

c.800BCE El Pilar founded

c.600BCE Izapa, Takalik Abaj and Chocolá become sites for cacao production

c.600– c.250BCE Heyday for Nakbé, sculpted stone and monumental architecture

c.400–c.300BCE Major building at Tikal

c.300BCE Maya establish hierarchical society ruled by kings and nobles

c.250BCE The earliest known written inscription in Mayan hieroglyphics

c.100BCE Teotihuacán is founded and becomes the region's cultural centre

c.100CE Construction of Teotihuacán's Pyramid of the Sun begins

c.100–c.300 Decline of the Olmecs

c.250–c.900 CLASSIC PERIOD

292 First stela in Tikal

378 Uaxactun is defeated by Tikal

c.430 Palenque is a major trading city

c.500 Uxmal is founded

c.500 Tikal becomes the first great Mayan city, greatly influenced by Teotihuacán

southwest, along the Usumacinta river system. The last known date at Bonampak appeared in 792, at Piedras Negras in 795 and at Palenque four years later. No more dates appeared at Yaxchilán after 808, following which the decline gathered momentum in the east and the north, into El Petén. The final recorded date at Quirigua was 810, at Copán 822, and at Caracol 859. By 909 end-dates for the important twenty-year periods known as katuns (see page 23) were no longer being recorded.

There are many theories as to what caused the rapid decline and abandonment of the Mayan kingdoms (see page 53), but the likeliest explanation is a combination of factors, the crucial ones being population growth and food shortages. The population of the southern lowlands reached its peak, of several millions, around 800, by which time the carrying capacity of the land, irrespective of the agricultural system, had probably been reached. The constant struggle (and competition) to find food meant the land must have been considerably overexploited. As we know from our own experience, the destruction of forests not only leads to soil erosion but can also change the climate – for example, by reducing the rainfall. While it is possible to make general assertions of this kind, it is likely that local circumstances differed, affecting each city-state in a distinctive way, though in each one the ruler would almost certainly have been held responsible for the deteriorating conditions that threatened the population's survival. This may have resulted in the breakdown of authority and created the conditions for rebellion. The heartland of Classic Maya civilization was worst affected and the outcome was apocalyptic and irreversible: groups of peasants were left to eke out a subsistence living among the jungle-clad ruins of cities erected as examples of the splendours of their forefathers' sophisticated civilization.

514 First inscribed date at Calakmul, which rises to rival Tikal in central area
562 Calakmul defeats Tikal
600–650 An unknown event destroys the civilization at Teotihuacán
683 Pacal dies and is buried at the Temple of Inscriptions in Palenque
695 Resurgent Tikal defeats Calakmul
700 Tikal's Temple VI is built
731 Stela A and stela B erected in Copán
740–750 Tikal's Temple of the Great Jaguar is built

c.750 Mayan alliances begin to fracture
c.800 Temple of Kukulkan (El Castillo) is begun at Chichén Itzá
800 Copán at its height
869 Construction ceases at Tikal
899 Tikal abandoned
900 Palenque and Copán sites abandoned
c.800–c.925 Classic period of Mayan history ends with the collapse of the southern lowland cities
909 Chichén Itzá records its final date

900–1521 POST-CLASSIC PERIOD
950–1000 Toltec occupy Chichén Itzá
1200 Quiché Maya settle
1200–1250 Chichén Itzá abandoned
1283 Mayapan becomes Yucatán capital
1441 Rebellion in Mayapan
1470 Kaqchikel Maya establish Iximché
1519–1521 Conquest of Mexico by Cortez
1524 Destruction of Iximché. Cortez crosses Yucatán peninsula
1839–1840 Stephens and Catherwood explore Chiapas and Yucatán

MASTER SCRIBES

The hieroglyphic writing system developed by the pre-Columbian Maya is radically different from the written language with which we in the West are familiar. The letters you are reading spell out words and have no other meaning, but Mayan glyphs, like the Kabbalistic interpretation of the letters of the Hebrew alphabet, have a sacred function, and the 850 or so characters carry meanings that link the Mayan people (especially their rulers) to the gods and the cosmos.

Although the glyphs were used for many ostensibly secular purposes – such as to record history and dynastic genealogies – they also offered scribes and readers alike a means of connecting with the divine. The writing system comprised logograms and syllabograms, respectively used to communicate meaning and to represent sounds. We now know that the Maya could write down everything they could say. Several Mayan languages were used, and it is thought that those who spoke Ch'olan and Tzeltalan invented the hieroglyphic system, while the Yucatec-speakers adopted it to write in their own language.

Bishop Diego de Landa Calderón (see pages 53–54) was the first to begin decoding the glyphs. He mistakenly assumed that each glyph could be represented by a letter in the Latin alphabet; also, that the glyphs, like letters, had sounds, whereas in fact they represent concepts. It was only in the middle of the twentieth century that the Mayan script began to be properly deciphered, when the Russian anthropologist Yuri Knorosov discovered that the writing was part phonetic and part ideographic, but based on syllables rather than on anything like a conventional alphabet. Building on the findings, other scholars were able to decode the stelae from Piedras Negras and Yaxchilán, revealing the history of some of the Mayan sites and the genealogy of their rulers.

INTO THE MINDS OF THE MAYA

An understanding of the glyphs reveals much about Mayan history, but just as interesting is the insight that the glyphs provide into Mayan mythology and astrology. The decoding gave access to the complicated calendars compiled from the Maya's astronomic observations over long periods of time, which contributed to the Maya's prophetic tradition.

The glyphs, usually carved, painted or written in grid-like cartouches on all kinds of surfaces, are read in a specific way. They are presented in parallel columns, and read downwards, left to right, starting at the top of the leftmost column and progressing to the bottom of the column, and then to the glyph at the top of the adjacent column to the right.

Further progress was made by Heinrich Berlin, whose work on monumental inscriptions revealed the existence

TIME AND NUMBERS are depicted by these glyphs carved in relief into a lintel at Yaxchilán. The animals represent periods of time, while the profiles of gods represent numbers. The glyphs combine to form a single date: 11 February 526ce in our Western calendar.

ITZAMNÁ SPEAKS TO A HUMMINGBIRD (right), a scene repeated on the left but with a human governor instead of Itzamná. The great deity is older and identified by a shell headdress and a flower-shaped mirror. The flower and the hummingbird are associated with blood and self-sacrifice, and here they have an additional link to the god through the word *itz*, which means "dew" and "nectar".

of an "emblem glyph". He noticed that the smaller parts were constant, but the main element changed according to the site where it was found. Thus, the emblem glyph was understood to represent a particular city, or dynasty, or the territory controlled by the ruler.

Unsurprisingly, the priceless "gift" of writing had its own deities. The high god Itzamná gave the skill to people, together with the calendars. However, some Mayan folk mythology credited this gift to the rabbit god, associated with the moon. Those who could write, the scribes, formed a privileged class, and the service they provided may at times have been shared with the priests. The scribes had their own dedicated deities, the most important of which were the howler monkey god, who was patron of all the arts, and the tonsured maize god, a patron god of the scribal arts in the Classic period.

So central was the hieroglyphic system, particularly with regard to numbers and mathematics, that the concept of number was built into the Maya's perception of an absolute god, known as Hunab Ku, the "Solitary God", whose name implied that he was the only divinity.

We can only speculate what information and wisdom might have been available to us if more of the codices had survived. Because of the loss of nearly all historic texts, our knowledge of ancient Mayan thought is limited and

THE MARVEL OF NUMBERS

As well as syllables, the glyphs were also used to represent a vigesimal (base twenty) number system, which provided the Maya with the means to develop their intricate calendars (see pages 22–27). That is the system found in the tables of the *Dresden Codex*, and it appears to have been the one used by priests and astronomers.

The Maya represented zero with the image of a shell (the *ximim*) or, alternatively, as half of a four-petalled flower, or an intact three-petalled flower. Zero was used to indicate the completion of a series in the Long Count calendar.

The number one is shown by a single dot • and the word *hum*. Two ••, three ••• and four •••• are also dots, but five is a bar ▬. From these basic blocks a complete numerical system was constructed. Thus ten is two bars ═ and thirteen is two bars with three dots above them.

The numbers one to twenty each had mythological associations and were represented by personified deities, with twenty itself having several glyphs, including. One represents Hunab Ku, the uncreated god; three the number of divisions in the vertical universe; four is the four cardinal points around the universal centre; five the ages of the sun (see page 112); and so on.

Arguably the two most significant numbers were thirteen and twenty, associated with short and longer periods of time. The origin of the use of these two numbers is uncertain, but thirteen has an esoteric association with Chac, the god of rain and fertility as well as the patron god of thirteen, and there are thirteen levels to the Upper World. The Maya counted time in twenty-year cycles (*katuns*). Twenty times thirteeen gives 260, which is the number of days required for mountain maize to grow and ripen.

can represent only a small portion of the complete picture. It is as if all that was known of the English-speaking world had to be based upon a couple of prayer books, an astronomy text and a portion of the Bible (see also boxes, pages 53 and 58).

Inevitably, suggestions have been made that Mayan writing may have been influenced by ancient Egyptian hieroglyphics. A far stronger argument can be made for the Mayan writing system having developed from the pictograms of neighbouring cultures, such as the Mixtec and Zapotec. There were clear influences from both the cultures that preceded the Maya, and those that developed contemporaneously, but there is no evidence that they were influenced by anything, or anyone, further afield than that. Where there are similarities, these owe their existence to parallel but independent development.

SACRED KEEPERS OF TIME

The measurement of time over long periods was a sacred commitment for the Maya. To understand and to record the interrelated movements of the sun, moon, Earth and planets meant that the Maya had to have a knowledge of advanced mathematics and a sophisticated understanding of what it was that they were observing. There is no evidence of how the Maya acquired these skills, though it is remarkable that everything was achieved by means of naked-eye observation.

THE CYCLES OF TIME

It is important to understand that the Maya's concept of time was cyclic, whereas the Western world perceives time as linear. However, for the purposes of recording history, the genealogies of the kings, the organization of trade and the planning of wars – in short, for all the practical purposes of everyday life – the Maya maintained a linear calendar. This, however, did not present the "reality" of time as the Maya understood it: their perception was shaped and conditioned by the notion that time can be measured in cycles, as can the movements of the planets of the solar system. Cyclic time is the concept upon which the prophecies are founded, and it is this that gives the prophecies their authority.

The Maya integrated their practical, linear calendar with others constructed according to the cyclic principle. If the human lifespan is thought of as a unit of time, it becomes clearer that linear time is a tiny portion of the greater wheel of time: part of the circumference of a circle that is so large we are unaware that the section of it on which we measure our existence is actually curved.

It is believed that the Maya developed at least twenty calendars, seventeen of which we have on record. Several of these were related to specific astronomical bodies: such as the sun and moon, or planets such as Earth, Venus and Mars. Other calendars were associated with the span of human life, and they dealt with biological, religious and social realities – with agricultural cycles, ceremonials and daily divinations. What the various calendars amounted to were different ways of recording the cyclic nature of time. To understand the Mayan calendric system and the prophecies it is necessary to know about two calendars in particular – the *tun* and *haab*, and the *tzolkin* – and how by interlocking (see diagram, page 24) they constitute larger cycles of time that culminate in the Long Count.

THE *TUN* YEAR AND THE *HAAB*

The calendar that most closely approximates the Gregorian calendar is the *tun* ("count"). It is better known as the "vague year" or "wandering year" of 360 days. Each day has an association with agriculture's creative cycle. Added to this 360-day *tun* year is a five-day intercalary period called the *wayeb* – an inauspicious time because the gods withdrew their support during this span. This full year of

365 days is called the *haab*. The winter solstice is when the *tun* year commences. (As explained in the tables, right and page 25, each of the twenty days and each of the eighteen months have a name, number and meaning.)

The basic Mayan calendric unit of time is the 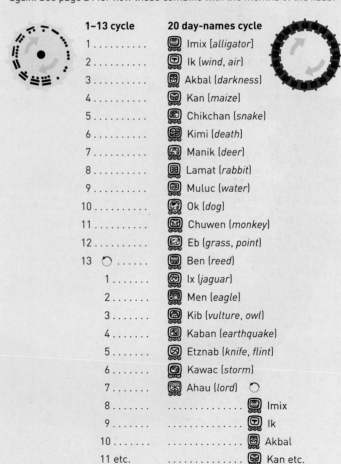 *kin* (day). Twenty *kin*s make a *winal* (month) and eighteen *winal*s make a *tun* of 360 days. Thereafter the units multiply in twenties: twenty *tun*s make a *katun* (7,200 days) and twenty *katun*s a *baktun* (144,000 days).

It is important to remember that our familiar Gregorian calendar consists of various multiple counts: one day in a cycle of seven (a week), a day in a numbered cycle of days (twenty-eight/twenty-nine, thirty or thirty-one), one in a cycle of twelve named months, one in a cycle of 365 days and one in a count of years that have elapsed since the birth of the Christian cycle (see also box, page 26).

THE *TZOLKIN* OR SACRED DAY CALENDAR

The *tzolkin* calendar means "count of days". This count is a divinatory, or sacred day, calendar based on the cycle of twenty named days (like a long week, each day of which is influenced or given character by a particular god) cycled thirteen times. The numbers twenty and thirteen, which have many symbolic and mythological associations, carry into multiples of much longer periods (see Long Count, page 27). The number thirteen's patron god is Chac, the deity of rain and fertility, and there are thirteen heavenly levels. Meanwhile, twenty is the number of elemental energies and the number shares its glyph with the moon.

TZOLKIN CALENDAR COMBINATIONS

By combining one of thirteen numbers with one of twenty day-names, it takes 260 days until the number 1 and the name Imix come together again. See page 24 for how these combine with the months of the *haab*.

1–13 cycle	20 day-names cycle
1	Imix [*alligator*]
2	Ik [*wind, air*]
3	Akbal [*darkness*]
4	Kan [*maize*]
5	Chikchan [*snake*]
6	Kimi [*death*]
7	Manik [*deer*]
8	Lamat [*rabbit*]
9	Muluc [*water*]
10	Ok [*dog*]
11	Chuwen [*monkey*]
12	Eb [*grass, point*]
13	Ben [*reed*]
1	Ix [*jaguar*]
2	Men [*eagle*]
3	Kib [*vulture, owl*]
4	Kaban [*earthquake*]
5	Etznab [*knife, flint*]
6	Kawac [*storm*]
7	Ahau [*lord*]
8	Imix
9	Ik
10	Akbal
11 etc.	Kan etc.

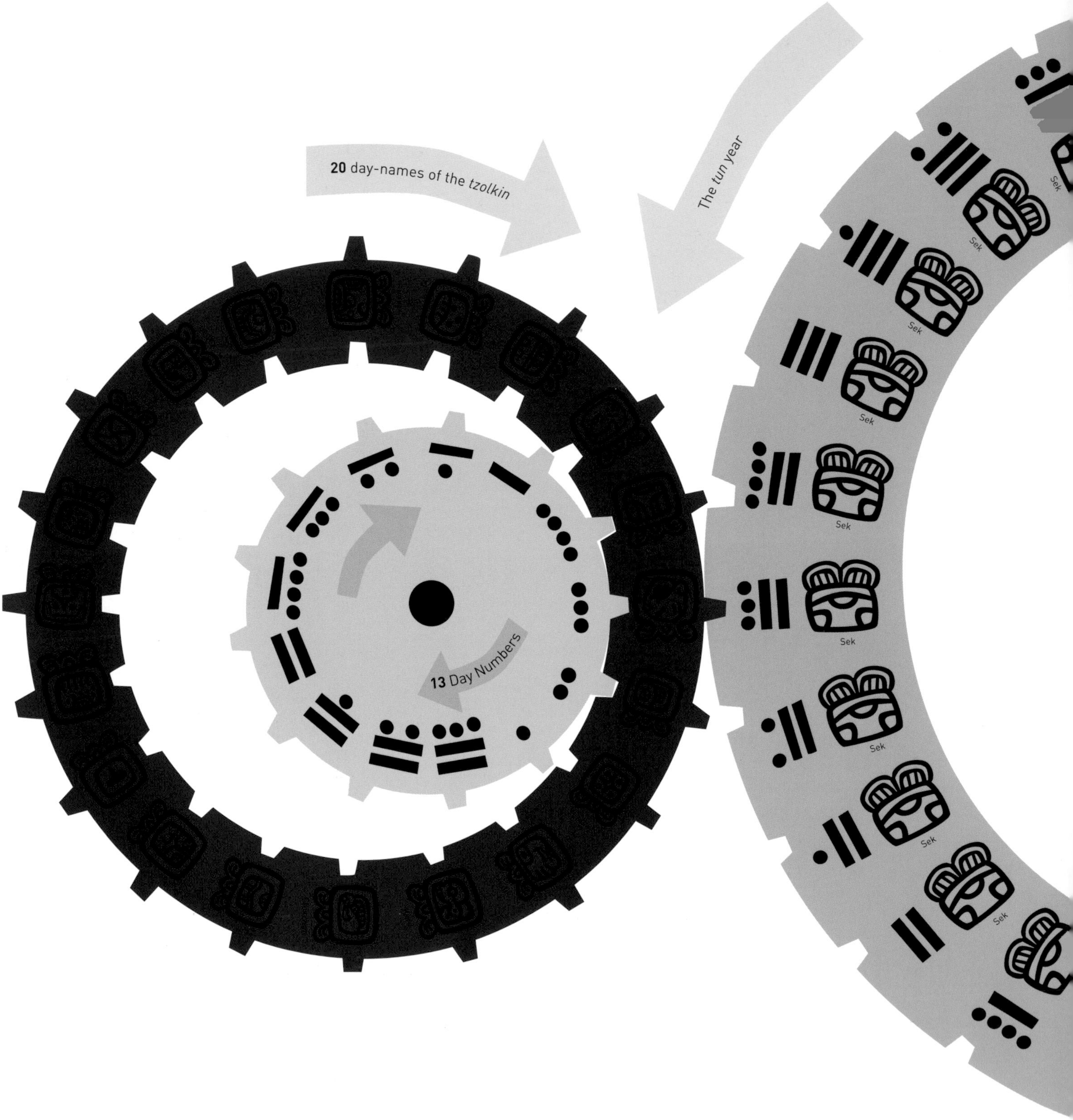

20 day-names of the tzolkin

The tun year

13 Day Numbers

Sek
Sek
Sek
Sek
Sek
Sek
Sek
Sek
Sek

THE MONTHS OF THE *HAAB* YEAR AND THEIR ASSOCIATIONS

The year began with Pop (guardian animal: the jaguar). During Pop the New Year ceremonies were held and households were ritually cleansed. Other months had their own festivals, such as that for the beekeepers in Sek or cocoa-growers in Muwan.

 MAK
to enclose, to cover

 POP
jaguar

 YAXKIN
new sun, red clouds

 KANKIN
yellow sun, ribs

 WO
night, blackness, frog

 MOL
to gather, water/clouds

 MUWAN
owl, falcon, hawk

 SIP
redness, stag

 CHEN
black storm, well, cave

 PAX
planting time, drum, arrow

 SOTZ
bat

 YAX
green storm

 KAYAB
turtle

 SEK
skull, bee

 SAC
white storm

 KUMKU
dark

 XUL
dog, termination

 KEH
red storm, forest, deer

 WAYEB
five unlucky days, spectre

Twenty multiplied by thirteen marries every combination of day-name and number, giving a count of 260 days before there is a repeat and the cycle begins again (see box, page 23). The period of 260 days is the time it takes for mountain maize to grow and ripen, and it also approximates the nine months of human gestation. The 260-day cycle has an echo in the nearly 26,000-year cycle of precession, which itself might be said to represent a 26,000-year cycle of biological unfolding – a type of spiritual gestation and birth – that the Earth and its consciousness-endowed life-forms undergo.

The *tzolkin* was thought of not simply as a short year, but as a sacred period that existed in its own right. The first thirteen of the twenty days are numbered as such (1–13), with the fourteenth day numbered as 1 again (the first day of a new cycle), the fifteenth as 2, and so on, through to the last of the twenty, which bears the number 7 (see box, page 23). For any given day to recur on the same number, the full cycle of 260 days must be completed. The day-names are the same as those in the twenty-day *winal*.

THE CALENDAR ROUND

For the first day of the 365-day *haab* to recur on the first day of the 260-day *tzolkin* cycle will take fifty-two *haab*s or seventy-three *tzolkin*s: this computation reveals a cycle of

THE LONG COUNT AND THE GREAT CYCLE

The Long Count expresses the number of days elapsed since the end of the last Great Cycle. The basis for the Long Count is a *tun*: a period of 360 solar days, or *kin*s. The *kin*s are grouped in twenties into eighteen *winal*s, or months. Twenty *tun*s (7,200 days) make a *katun*. Twenty *katun*s (144,000 days) make a *baktun*. Thirteen *baktun*s (1,872,000 days) is a Great Cycle.

Presented with Wednesday 4 July 2012, Westerners will understand what is represented, from the fourth day in a cycle of seven, known as a week, through to 2012 as a count of the number of years since the birth of Jesus initiated a Christian cycle of time. Mayan Long Count dates are written from the left, beginning with *baktun*s: 4 July 2012 becomes 12.19.19.9.10 –

representing 12 *baktun*, 19 *katun*, 19 *tun*, 9 *winal*, 10 *kin*. The Calendar Round is 3 Oc, 13 Sek (see the day and month glyphs below and page 25). It is calculated that this current Great Cycle began in 3114BCE and will complete in December 2012.

18,980 days, known as the "calendar round". It is likely to have existed in Mesoamerica since c.2500BCE, which makes it one of the oldest calendars in existence.

The "calendar round" was thought adequate for marking specific days and months, or longer periods of time, for recording dates, events and the span of a person's life. As with the *wayeb*, with which the *haab* year finishes, the end of the "calendar round" was a threatening period of darkness. The Maya could never be sure the gods would allow another cycle, and therefore important rituals were enacted, such as adding a new level to a pyramid or carving a new inscription to situate an event in time.

THE LONG COUNT CALENDAR

The Long Count is a period of thirteen *baktun*s, which is 1,872,000 days (5,200 *tun* years and approximately 5,126 solar years). The present Long Count era began on 13 August 3114BCE (also referred to as the date of "the birth of Venus") and it will end on 21 December 2012. On 22 December a new cycle will begin. Scholars calculated this by correlating more recent Mayan dates (from inscriptions) with the Gregorian and Julian calendars. The calculations are complex and the start date is not accepted by all Mayanist scholars (the range is 11–13 August).

Because the Long Count has a beginning and an end it provides a linear view of time, enabling the Maya to record history, organize the present and plan the future. More importantly, astronomical events such as eclipses and Venus transits could be marked.

The dates in the Long Count are always numbered in the same sequence: *baktun*, *katun*, *tun*, *winal* and *kin*. Once the thirteen *baktun*s of the current Long Count have been completed, by 21 December 2012, the date will be represented as 13.0.0.0.0.

Many of the Long Count inscriptions include glyphs known as the lunar series, and there are eight such series. These glyphs record a date in the lunar calendar (the Maya had one called the Tun-Uc, see page 98), the name of the current lunar month and the number of days that have passed since the new moon. The number of days of the lunar month are variously indicated as being twenty-nine or thirty. The *Dresden Codex* contains a lunar series and provides the most detailed charts and accounts of the cycles of Venus, showing not only the dates of it rising and setting as the morning and evening star but also the dates on which the planet will transit across the face of the sun (see page 106).

Overarching the calendars is the phenomenon of precession (see page 86). The rotation and imperceptible wobble of the Earth on its axis as it journeys around the sun means that the heavenly location of a constellation when viewed from Earth will gradually change over time. It is this change of viewpoint that astronomers call "precession". There is a relationship between this and galactic synchronization: an astronomical event that will bring the Earth and the planets of the solar system into an alignment with a point in the Milky Way. This alignment recurs approximately every 26,000 years and it will happen on 21 December 2012 (see pages 84–87).

THE POWER OF PROPHECY

To the modern mind, the concept of prophecy might conjure up imagery of ancient Old Testament scripture, the cryptic, slightly sinister projections of Nostradamus, or controversial figures from more recent centuries said to possess "the gift" and to have a special insight. Reflecting a culture that was preoccupied with the cycles of time, Mayan foretelling of the future was quite different from any of these.

Mayan prophets were honoured in their society and belonged to a special class of the priesthood known as the *chilam balam*, or "jaguar prophets". These individuals acted as channels for messages sent from the gods, and those they received while in a trance state were recorded in books. The most important single source is the *Book of Chilam Balam of Chumayel*, which is a collection of nine smaller manuscripts named after their towns of origin (for example, Tizimin). Recorded in Yucatec, using European script, the texts were probably transcribed from older hieroglyphic codices.

THE CHARACTER OF TIME

Study of the prophetic texts reveals the importance of the framework provided by the ancient Mayan calendars. It is clear that the key to appreciating the power of Mayan prophecy is to understand that each unit of time – *kin*s, *winal*s, *tun*s, *katun*s, *baktun*s – has a form of personality. The resultant prophecies fall into one of several categories.

A day prophecy was a prognostication more likely to have been given by a diviner, or *ah-kinyah*, than a *chilam*. Almanacs based on the 260-day *tzolkin* were widespread and influential among the Maya. Both the *Dresden Codex* and the *Madrid Codex* provide a great deal of esoteric and astronomical information on the moon and Venus, which was used for this sort of day-by-day divinatory purpose. Every day was lucky or unlucky for certain trades, more or less auspicious for particular activities (such as beekeeping or hunting), and so on. Today, in Yucatán and Guatemala, such ancient practices can still be found, called "day-keeping". To find a favourable date for a marriage or a business transaction, or for advice on an agricultural project, the day-keeper is consulted.

Historically, the cyclic structure of the calendars pivot most significantly around the twenty-year *katun*s, and that is where the field of genuine prophecy is represented most strongly. A *katun* of the same name recurs after approximately 256 years and the principle of circular time implies that whenever this happens in the cycle, similar events will occur. The prophecies made were rooted in this principle, which was deeply embedded in the lives of the Maya. Events recounted in the chronicles reveal how this belief could influence history. It is striking that many of the upheavals in Mayan history occurred in 4 Ahau or 8 Ahau.

THE JAGUAR THRONE in front of the Palace of the Governor at Uxmal (see also page 159). Both rulers and priests named themselves after this revered big cat.

KINGS, COMMONERS AND DEITIES

The role of king did not emerge in Mayan society until the late Pre-Classic period, c.300BCE–c.100CE. It was an office that grew out of an elite hereditary class of lords known as the *ahau*, or *ajaw*. Ahau is also the last day of the ritual calendar, a day dedicated to the sun god Kinich Ahau, who was a manifestation of the supreme god Itzamná. The kings thus assumed absolute, even divine, attributes. *Ahau* could denote lord, ruler, king or leader, but whatever its specific meaning, *ahau* was the term used by the Maya for the absolute ruler of a city-state. Because of this association with the sun god, his glyph was often part of the king's name, or title – Kinich Janaab Pacal, for example. The glyph for the name sometimes carried a prefix *kubul*, meaning "holy". The king's association with the jaguar gods was also significant, because he was assumed to share some of their characteristics.

The king was at the apex of a rigid social hierarchy. Provincial governors were usually nobles drawn from the ruling family, and they enjoyed absolute authority within their own administrations. Below the governor were the heads of towns and villages, a lower-ranked class of nobility who were not of royal blood. Orbiting around this pyramidal structure were clearly defined groups of lords and priests. The lords were military leaders, each with a

THE RISE AND FALL OF MAYAN CITY-STATES

Each Mayan kingdom consisted of a capital city, called an *ajawil*, headed by its lord or king. The region around the city would have included a number of lesser towns. Many of the present Mayan World Heritage Sites, such as Chichén Itzá, Palenque, Tikal and Copán, were once the capitals of their states. Most of these cities were at their height toward the end of the ninth century CE, long before the Spanish encountered them, though it is believed that Mayan political structures had changed little. The Classic and Post-Classic history of the Maya is a story of near-perpetual rivalry and warfare between the various city-states, the rise to prominence and then decline of particular cities, and the ending of dynasties and the founding of new ones. Wars were driven by the ambition of a ruler to increase the size of his kingdom, the pressure to expand territorially because of the demands made on agriculture by a growing population, and the constant need for slaves and sacrificial victims.

STATUS AND POWER was symbolized among the Maya by polychrome ceramic vessels. Dating to c.600–800CE, examples such as this were used by the elite and are found as offerings in rich burials. The scene here represents the delivery of tribute to a seated lord, identifiable through his ornate turban.

command of their own, supported by a "staff" who provided for them from land that they farmed but did not own – a system similar to feudalism in medieval Europe. A lower class comprised farmers, artisans, tradesmen and merchants who were taxed and had to be available to serve during wartime. The spoils of war included slave families, who could work out their servitude and gain their freedom.

The entire lower social structure was based on a form of clanship in which clan chiefs were assigned custodianship but were not given absolute authority. As custodians, the clan chiefs were responsible for the well-being of their own people and for ensuring the security of the territories they occupied.

CONNECTING WITH THE GODS

Mayan society made no distinction between the observable, tangible world and the invisible world of the spirit. Mayan religion, cosmology and ritual were outward and visible signs of an inward, invisible reality. The invisible was represented in carvings, sculptures, masks and so on. Shaman-priests, notably the *chilam balam* prophets, possessed the special gifts to act as intermediaries between these worlds. So too did the nobles by means of the bloodletting auto-sacrifices they practised during their quests to summon the Vision Serpent (see page 75).

The human rulers of cities appear to have formed part of the hierarchical Mayan pantheon of gods. The rulers impersonated gods and goddesses – using masks and costumes – during celebrations and rituals, and they claimed divinity as part of their legitimation of earthly power. A ruler presented himself to the public as a manifestation of the deities, with an elaborated form of dress that emphasized his wealth and status.

The people looked to the ruler as the guarantor of social stability. In turn this stability was founded on effective agriculture, trade and the successful prosecution of wars with rival states. As each of these was dependent on the gods, the king was held responsible for holding earthly and cosmic forces in the correct balance.

A POWERFUL PANTHEON

A large pantheon of gods is characteristic of animistic religion and there are several reasons for this. Firstly, it can be seen as an insurance policy, a way of ascribing responsibility for every contingency in life, for individuals as well as the wider community. Secondly, it is a way of establishing a series of relationships with the natural world that are potentially favourable to the society in question. Thirdly, accumulating a large pantheon is a response to the full range of fear-provoking phenomena, from natural forces such as storms, earthquakes and volcanoes to abstractions such as the darkness of night, the immensity of the universe and the indispensability of the sun. Believing that so many different things are controlled by gods offers humans hope that they can obtain some influence over hugely powerful forces that both sustain and threaten life. Fourthly, a team of gods, once established, provides the means of shaping and controlling society on the principle "as above, so below". Wherever a large pantheon has existed, both the pantheon and the coexisting human society have tended to be hierarchical, even if the mortal incumbents changed with some regularity. The Maya's divine pantheon and social organization exhibit these characteristics.

In the twenty-one prophecies that follow (pages 48–169) many different gods and goddesses make an appearance, from gods of particular reptiles to those

ITZAMNÁ – THE PRINCIPAL GOD

 Although Quetzalcoatl–Kukulcan is the most familiar of the old Mesoamerican gods (see pages 68–75), it is the creator god Itzamná who occupies the place at the top of the Maya's divine hierarchy. He can be depicted with snake-like features, reflecting the fact that in Mayan cosmology the serpent symbolized heaven, Earth and the afterworld. As creator god he embodies these aspects in his person.

Religion and mythology are never fixed in time, and in their most vital manifestations they evolve. If there is no growth, it may be because the religion has become stultified, or held within a particular form at a particular time by conservatism. To follow the Maya from their early Pre-Classic to their late Post-Classic culture is to sense a process: the emergence and dominance of a supreme god, heralding a move from polytheism to monotheism.

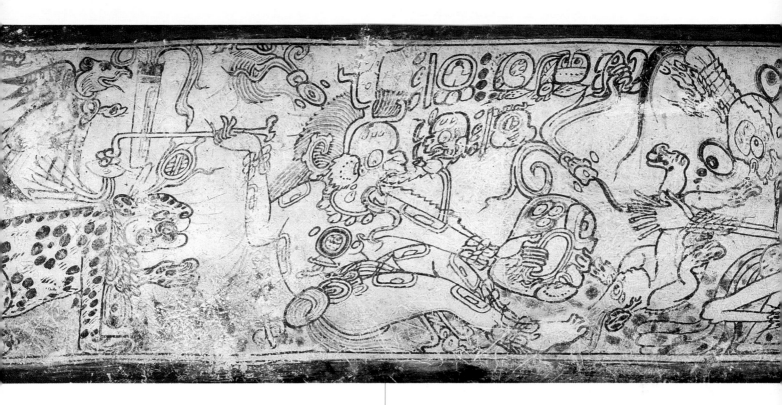

CHAC AND YUM CIMIL IN THE UNDERWORLD welcome an elite baby into the afterlife. Yum Cimil is skeletal; Chac can be recognized by his stone axe and the lightning flashing from his mouth. The infant, with jaguar paws, ears and a tail, is at the moment of its passing being reborn as the jaguar god of the Underworld.

associated with celestial bodies, although it should be appreciated that the Mayan pantheon is complex and the gods can be classified by their functions only loosely, because many of them have different manifestations and roles overlap.

GODS OF LIFE, GODS OF DEATH

There are generations of creation gods whose story is told in the *Popul Vuh*. The jaguar gods have various names, such as Bird Jaguar and Shield Jaguar: these gods are the principal *nahual*, or double, of kings and shamans, contactable by means of hallucinatory rituals. The cult of the jaguar gods was centred on the tropical forests, the natural habitat of the great predatory feline, the jaguar. The maize god Yum Kaax is portrayed as an attractive youth, and his story is central to Mayan mythology because maize was the staple diet of the Maya as well as the substance out of which the first humans were made. A tonsured form of the maize god doubled as patron of the scribes. The deities of weather include Chac, the god of rain and lightning, and Huracan (also known as Heart of Sky), the god of violent and sudden changes reflected in the wind, storms and fires.

THEATRE OF BLOOD is an apt name for the spectacle that the ballcourt provided for its spectators – a gory drama played out as a ritual game that might last for days and may often have ended in the death of several of the participants. This is the ballcourt at Copán (see also pages 42–43).

Xibalba, the Underworld of the Maya, has a rich and complex iconography. The actual death god, Yum Cimil (or God A), was said to rule the lowest region of Xibalba's nine lower worlds, with nine corresponding lords of the night. Yum Cimil was the patron of the day Kimi and the number ten. His animal *nahual*s were birds: the muan and owl.

A similar death god, known as Buluk Chabtan (or God F), is related to war and human sacrifice. He differs from the god of death in that his realm is specifically the violent death of the battlefield and the sacrificial altar. Associated with the number eleven, Buluk Chabtan had a female manifestation as the negative form of Ix Chel, the rainbow goddess and bride of Itzamná (see box, page 32), but here acting as a bearer of misfortune.

Xibalba was also home to a dozen lords of death, the most senior of whom were Hun Came (One Death) and Vucub Came (Seven Death). A cycle in the *Popol Vuh* tells of a memorable encounter between the Hero Twins and these two senior lords of death.

That story reflects the complicated relationship that Mayan rulers had with death and the death god. Rulers were believed to be descendants of the gods, and when a ruler was captured he might be held as a prisoner for months or even years – in order to be sacrificed on an

THE MESOAMERICAN BALLGAME

It is thought that this ancient game has been played across Mesoamerica since 3000BCE. The size of the court varies, but all have a long, narrow, rectangular shape, set between sloping or vertical walls with wider end zones. Each team usually had five players, who played using a latex rubber ball that may have weighed nearly seven pounds (3kg). No records have been found of the rules of the game, but it is thought that the ball had to be kept in play between marked boundaries, and could only be struck using particular parts of the body. It is doubtful if the game was ever played purely as a sport: instead it seems to have been a form of contest used to settle relatively minor local disputes concerning boundaries or trade.

At the temple complexes the game had a much more macabre aspect, incorporating cosmic symbolism. The ball represented the sun, and the game was played (possibly two-a-side) as the conflict between night and day. This meaning could be emphasized by the orientation of the court to a particular point on the horizon.

Each ballcourt also had a specially marked spot from which Xibalba could be accessed. This enabled the game to be played as a re-enactment of the *Popul Vuh* drama of the Hero Twins, Hunahpú and Xbalanqué, descending to Xibalba to vanquish death. In this mode the stakes were life and death, with at least some of the losing participants being offered as sacrifices at the end. Evidence from a carved relief at a ballcourt site shows a winner holding the head of one of his defeated opponents.

important occasion. Lord Siebal was kept alive for twelve years in order to be coerced into a ritual suicide at a conjunction of Venus. Whether by violence or natural causes, a king faced with death was expected to engage and outwit the gods of death, thereby gaining immortality for himself by taking the form of a celestial body.

The tussle with death is a common theme in world mythology, and when the Mayan Hero Twins descend to Xibalba to exact revenge for Hun Hunahpu by vanquishing death (see page 133), they are subjected to a series of ordeals. The two pass through six deadly houses: the Dark House, the Rattling or Cold House, the Jaguar House, the Bat House (home to the dreaded *camazotz* bat, capable of decapitation), the Razor House and the Hot House.

The drama of mythology was the theme of an extraordinary contest called the ballgame (see box, above). Played earnestly in the manner of a competitive sport, the ballgame was a ritualized re-enactment of the conflict between life and death. The Underworld could be accessed through a portal in the ballcourt itself.

FEEDING THE GODS

The great temple complexes, at places such as Chichén Itzá and Tikal, were served by an order of full-time priests. (This order may have been introduced to the Maya by the Toltec at the same time as the deity Quetzalcoatl–Kukulcan – see page 69.) During the Classic period it is thought that some or all of the duties of the priests were commandeered by the ruling elite as a way of strengthening its authority. However, a distinction has to be made between what might be termed the ceremonial aspects of a priest's duties, such as maintaining the calendars and observing the rituals ordered by them, and the unique spiritual service that was offered. Even if the practical responsibilities of the priesthood were taken over by the elite, the role of the shaman-priest as a vision-quest intermediary between the community and the gods must have remained unaffected.

The term for priest, *ah kin*, means "he of the sun" or "priest of the calendar" (some of them specialized in the *katun* cycles – see page 28). Each temple had its own priesthood, ordered in a strict hierarchy with the high priest in the main temple and the lower orders serving in the towns and villages. There was also a female priesthood whose high priestess had to be of royal blood. Known as *ix men*, the priestesses' duties included the sacred arts of medicine, the preparation of herbal cures, and midwifery. In this capacity they related to Ixchel (meaning "Lady Rainbow"), the important Mayan goddess who was the patron of fertility, pregnancy and childbirth. In some rituals of purification, still practised today by priestesses in the Yucatán and Guatemala, the moon goddess is invoked (see also pages 96–101).

BLOOD: THE WELLSPRING OF LIFE

Nearly all the rituals central to Mayan civilization involved sanctification through the shedding of blood, the sacred liquid of life. From weddings to births, the giving of blood expressed piety and summoned the gods. Sacrifice was the core of Mayan religion: besides humans, all kinds of creatures were used, including turkeys, jaguars, dogs, quail, serpents, hummingbirds and even butterflies. The creation mythology in the *Popul Vuh* makes it clear that the gods had to be thanked continually and given sustenance for having created human beings. If people neglected this, all manner of ills might befall their villages and cities.

Different gods had different requirements. At Chichén Itzá many people were sacrificed to the rain god Chac (see pages 143–144 and box, page 147). Among the Quiché Maya, Tohil was revered as the giver of fire who required as recompense human hearts that were still beating. Four priests would assist the ruler-priest in holding a human victim, painted in sacrificial blue, across an altar stone called a *chacmool* (see illustration, page 145), before the heart was cut out of the chest and offered to the god. Other forms of killing included beheading, disembowelling and being bound, then rolled down the steps of a pyramid.

HUMAN AND ANIMAL SACRIFICE depicted on a vase. The sacrificer is a ruler who is holding a macaw, which may be the next victim, while an attendant readies a jaguar. Blood-spotted garments are worn by everyone in attendance except the human victim, who lies dying upon the sacrificial stone. Blood-saturated cloth was burned in a brazier to create smoke, which was necessary for the gods to be able to consume the blood.

A form of non-fatal, ritual auto-sacrifice known as bloodletting was also practised widely by members of the ruling dynasties. A man drew blood by piercing his genitals, and a woman her tongue or earlobes. As with fatal sacrifice, the act acknowledged that the gods had shed their own blood in the process of creating the first humans. The perforating regalia of bloodletting was often buried with the dead as funerary charms, forming part of a sacred bundle that was laid over the body's pelvic region. For the Maya, bloodletting was thought to be a means of revitalizing life-energy: a ritual way of returning to the gods the life they had given to people – a reciprocation that helped to maintain the balance of the universe. In turn, the gods themselves were believed to give their blood to maintain the order of the cosmos.

Many cultures throughout history have practised human sacrifice to appease the gods. In the same way that we are anxious about illness, redundancy, terrorism or the pressure to make something of one's life, the Maya felt threatened by the fragility of life itself, because of the dangers that loomed from crop failure, famine, drought, war, being taken prisoner, and so on. Many of these threats were related to specific gods, who had to be kept happy. However, the Maya's principal fear was that time would end. To avert that tragedy they felt driven to try to control the powers that held life in such a fragile balance.

REPRESENTING THE COSMOS

Although it is probably untrue that the Maya attempted an architectural model of the universe, the design of certain buildings, and the planning of towns, seems intended to represent aspects of the cosmos: the most obvious examples are tall structures as mountains. Mayan sites, however, were not just religious and ritual complexes – they had to serve as everyday centres of commerce.

The Mayan world consisted not just of the Earth and its surrounding water: there was a dark Underworld and a star-filled heaven. Once the sun had set in the west it was believed to enter the Underworld until it reappeared at dawn in the east. The Maya noticed that the points on the horizon of the rising and setting of the sun changed during the course of a year between midsummer and midwinter. They also noticed that the rising and setting of the sun was halfway between those points in early spring and autumn (see also pages 41–44). These points of the sun the Maya identified with a different direction.

The basic components of any site's layout were the cardinal points, each of which was associated with a *bacab*, the mythological sky-bearers, and a colour. The centre is occupied by the sacred ceiba tree, a link between the annual high and low points of the sun and an earthly form of the mighty World Tree that was believed to provide the

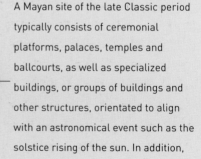

SYMBOLS IN STRUCTURES

A Mayan site of the late Classic period typically consists of ceremonial platforms, palaces, temples and ballcourts, as well as specialized buildings, or groups of buildings and other structures, orientated to align with an astronomical event such as the solstice rising of the sun. In addition, some sites had dedicated observatories such as El Caracol at Chichén Itzá (see page 67). At larger sites such as Tikal several complexes may be connected by ritual causeways. Also at Tikal, the twin pyramids, with their observation platforms open to the sky, are a notable example of Mayan architectural cosmology, with the nine doors representing the nine levels of Xibalba.

A city's plaza could represent the surface of the Underworld. When flooded during the rainy season it reproduced the primordial sea that once covered the Earth. The Mayan word for a stela was *te tun*, meaning "stone tree", which suggests that a stela was symbolic of the ceiba tree, the Mayan *axis mundi*.

EDZNA'S MAIN TEMPLE is its most prominent building because it is erected on top of a platform 130ft (40m) high, which gives it a commanding overview of the area. Located in modern-day Campeche, Mexico, the site was settled for about 2,000 years (c.400BCE–c.1500CE). Dates inscribed on stelae at Edzna range from 435CE to 810CE. During the Classic period it may have been a vassal of Calakmul.

connecting axis between the thirteen upper levels (each with its own god), the Earth and the nine levels of the Underworld (also each with its own god). The ceiba tree was linked with the colours blue and green.

Each cardinal direction has its own glyph, name and colour: *lahkin*, the east, is red; *xaman*, the north, is white; *chikin*, the west, is black; and *nolh*, the south, is yellow. Each of these four directions and colours was integrated with the calendars, moving through the twenty day-names in a counter-clockwise direction. Thus, the four directions assume a calendric significance because each direction is associated with five particular days within the twenty-day cycle. In astronomical references the east is identified with Venus, the north with the North Star, the west with death, and the south with the sun. These quaternate formulae have their origin in the *Popul Vuh* where the Earth is described as set out like a maize field (see page 95).

In courtyard groups of buildings and palace complexes the Maya appear to have sought to place their structures harmoniously into the natural environment. By carefully incorporating alignments with celestial bodies many elements of the Maya's man-built world seem to reflect their interest in the cycles of time.

A "WHITE ROAD", or *sak be*, at Labna runs through this arch. These straight road networks physically linked urban centres with surrounding areas, but they may also have had a conceptual meaning. Whereas the Milky Way and then the ceiba tree provide networks of macro-routes for the transmission of divine energy, the *sak be* may have been micro-routes completing the sacred circuit.

The Maya's obsession with making the cosmos concrete goes beyond the immediate precincts of their major sites. Their sense of the sacred was profound, and virtually everything was endowed with a spirit. As we have seen, the Maya endeavoured to mirror this in the built environment, but they were aware that the real, potent realms of the gods transcended the material world.

The various urban complexes were interconnected by what are called *sacbeob*, or *sak be* ("white roads" – a name they also gave to the Milky Way). These raised causeways provided a straight-line route between the remoter areas of the sites and the more important locations. However, something of a mystery attaches itself to the *sak be*. At sites such as Coba there are more than sixteen causeways, and there is no clear reason why they were constructed: one runs for several miles only to lead to a site that seems inconsequential. It is probable that the roads would have been used to facilitate trade but they could also have served ritual and ceremonial purposes.

In Europe many people believe in invisible ley lines that connect sacred places such as henges and barrows. A similar notion exists among Australia's Aborigines, who attach much significance to the spirit energy of places. It

ANIMISTIC WORLDS OF SPIRIT POWER

The Maya believed that just about everything was imbued with spiritual power. They understood that the world is a community of living beings, only some of them human. Accordingly, the gods could take either animal or human form.

The Maya believed that the sun, moon, planets and stars, whose movements marked the passage of time, were themselves "star walker" deities assuming "astromorphic" forms. Whatever form it took, every thing was possessed of a vital form called *ik*, meaning "wind" or "breath".

The clear, unpolluted Mayan night skies enabled them to keep the celestial bodies constantly in view. In this way they felt at one with the nature gods, such as Chac, the god of rain. The remainder of their pantheon they had to make equally visible, which they achieved through architecture (and its sculptures and relief carvings) and glyphs – huge galleries of art that were a necessary incarnation of the gods.

seems likely that the Maya had a similar concept of sacred connectivity. Particular locations, such as caves and mountains, were thought to be especially significant and powerful. It has been proposed that the *sak be* may link sites with points on the horizon that are of astronomical significance. The "white roads", of course, share the same name as the Milky Way, perhaps making them all cosmological roads travelled by the shamans and all who participated in the rituals performed along those roads.

ARCHAEOASTRONOMY

The location of particular buildings, and the alignment of structures and stelae, was determined primarily by horizon astronomy. Crucially important things happen on the horizon – namely, the rising and setting of stars, the sun, the moon and the planets. Of special importance is what is termed the heliacal rising and setting – that is, the first appearance of a star or planet when it becomes visible before sunrise, or its last appearance after the sun has set. Aligning a building, or a group of buildings toward any of these points allowed the Maya to measure the length of the tropical year, as well as all the other elements of their calendars – even the period of precession (see box, page 86).

From a fixed point or latitude on Earth – and for a period amounting to approximately a human lifetime – a star will rise in one azimuth (the horizontal angle of a

COPÁN – THE FOREST OF TREE-STONES

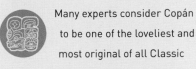

Many experts consider Copán to be one of the loveliest and most original of all Classic period population centres. The city is located above the Río Copán, a tributary of the Río Motagua, in western Honduras. The kingdom of Copán, under the name Xukpi, which means "Corner-Bundle", was at its height from the fifth to the ninth century CE, with its golden age somewhere between. After Copán had been abandoned, the jungle caused considerable damage but the site remains remarkable, with a great plaza, temple-pyramids, a large and well-preserved ballcourt, and an extraordinary series of portrait stelae.

Of all the man-made elements at Copán, probably the most striking are the portraits and sculptures that adorn the façades and entrances of the buildings. There are twenty stelae and fourteen altars, carved with images of the rain god, the maize god, and many other deities. The altars would have

been where bloodletting was carried out in full view of an awe-struck public.

To the south of the ballcourt is Temple 26, which was completed in the late Classic period and is famous for its sixty-three stone steps, the risers of which are covered in a text of around 2,500 glyphs. The text, which is reminiscent of the names or battle honours on a Western war memorial, commemorates the most prestigious sacrifices and the dynastic history of six of Copán's rulers. The steps were created in two phases, initiated by 18 Rabbit (reigned 695–738) and completed by Smoke Shell (reigned 749–763), who is depicted on stelae M and N (at temples 26 and 11, respectively).

The site appears to have been arranged on a north–south axis, which may have symbolic meaning. The cardinal direction north was associated with the heavenly realm and royalty. One inference that can be drawn from this is political: that royal authority at Copán

was sanctioned by supernatural power. Many alignments elsewhere map the path of the sun between sunrise and sunset, symbolizing the heavens and the Underworld. The portrait stelae of most rulers at Copán are located in the northern enclosures. This can be interpreted to mean that those rulers were metaphorically transported to the heavens, where they joined their royal ancestors and the midday sun as emblems of strength and authority.

Mayan civilization excelled at achieving extraordinary levels of meaning in architecture and art. The incorporation of mythological and astronomical themes – honouring the gods, earthly rulers and the cosmos – was accomplished on an enormous, spectacular and all-inclusive scale.

SMOKE SHELL, COPÁN'S 15TH RULER, is depicted here on Stela N, which was erected on the north side of Temple 11 in 761CE. Smoke Shell, also known as Smoke Squirrel, was responsible for completing the famous "hieroglyph stairway".

compass bearing) and set in another. However, the point on the horizon where the sun rises and sets varies according to the time of the year. The moon also follows a fixed pattern of rising and setting (which presented the Maya with problems when they tried to create a calendar that reconciled the cycles of the moon and the sun), as does Venus with a complex cycle of its own (see pages 102–109). Remarkably, without access to sophisticated technology, the Maya became aware of these movements and relationships, which they recorded and computed, before planning their sites in accordance with them.

ARCHITECTURE ADORNED

We have seen the extent to which all the important buildings of a Mayan ceremonial site were decorated by relief carvings, sculptures, murals and hieroglyphs, each serving a religious or ritual function, or recording and celebrating the life of a king or a dynasty.

An additional function of the artist, whether as scribe or as illustrator, was to record significant history, triumph in war, prisoners and their sacrifice. It is not known whether any of this work was intended purely to beautify a building or a space, such as a public plaza. It is believed that the "decorations" were mostly functional and that any sense of beauty was expressed in the harmonious way that the space itself was organized and in the impression of proportion provided by the architectural forms.

No doubt each kingdom had its own vernacular preferences for its art and architecture. An interesting example of variations in regional styles is the work of the artists of Copán, who are thought to be the first in Mesoamerica to make images of legged serpents. The Chichén Itzá serpents, shown from the front rather than from the side, are derived from the Copán originals. Outside this ceremonial and public form of art, there was more scope for individualism: the Maya produced sculptures, paintings, pottery, ceramics, textiles, jewelry, bone-carvings and weavings (few historic textiles have survived, but contemporary weaving flourishes and is often highly traditional – see illustration, opposite).

CONQUEST AND RENEWAL

With the collapse and abandonment of the principal Mayan sites by c.900CE, Mayan civilization regrouped in the north and by the time the Spanish arrived 600 years later had become centred on Chichén Itzá and Mayapan.

The Spanish Conquest had a devastating effect on Mayan culture. Inevitably, Roman Catholicism gradually infiltrated the Maya's indigenous cosmology and mythologies. Even those few codices that survived appear to have reinterpreted the prophecy of the coming of foreigners and new religion, and the return of a supreme being, in Christian terms (see pages 50–55 and pages 68–75, respectively). The coming of the new religion did not result in the sudden conversion of the Maya and the abandonment of their indigenous religion. Instead there was a gradual assimilation of the new by the old, leading to a form of syncretic faith. The essential functions of

Mayan religion supported the survival of Mayan cultural identity, the hierarchical structure of their society, and a reciprocal relationship with the environment and the universe. As the Trinitarian God, the cult of Mary, and the saints of the new religion were adopted, the Maya adapted them so that these functions continued to be served. In this way the Christian saints combined with Mayan ancestors and "earth lords" to become essential aspects of a thriving and local modern Mayan identity. This combination of Catholicism and ancient Mayan belief is the dominant religion today.

Mayan cosmology also survives, although the veneration of saints seems to have largely displaced the worship of nature gods. The planetary deities, especially the sun and moon, remain important, but the sun is a manifestation of God while the moon is a manifestation of

CEREMONIAL SHIRTS, known as *huipil* ("blouse"), have been woven by Mayan women for centuries and the craft remains strong today. This example is from the village of Santa Magdalena, Chiapas, Mexico. The *huipil* is embellished with intricate designs that incorporate symbols of flowers, gods, amphibians, vultures and other things of mythological importance. The repetition and placement of the designs create a cosmological interrelationship between the wearer and the imagery, and, ultimately, a harmonious unity among the concepts symbolized.

the Virgin Mary. In rural areas, spirits are still believed to inhabit the forests, rivers, caves and *cenote*s, and the sacredness of mountains is acknowledged by the sacrifices of animals at wayside shrines.

In some instances the old gods are combined with a Christian saint to create a fresh manifestation of an old deity. An example of this is Maximón, a popular post-Columbian Mayan deity who blends aspects of the Christian San Simón with those of a Mayan god. The story varies from town to town, but the most famous Maximón is the one found in Santiago Atitlán, Guatemala: a mix of Jesus, Simon the Zealot and Judas Iscariot. Maximón's multiple identities allow him to serve the different needs of various communities in the same way that some of the old Mayan gods did.

Within this syncretic matrix, other aspects of the original religion survive, such as spirit guides who take the form of animals, fish or birds. Augury is still practised in Guatemala, and communities there still live by the ancient calendars. The ancient Mayan *cuch*, or burden ritual, provides another fascinating example of adaptation. This ritual celebrated fertility, or the changing agricultural seasons, and was conducted to ensure the continuation of life. A deer or stag fight was held that concluded with the sacrifice of the animal. In the post-Conquest drama a bullfight replaces the deer fight.

Irrespective of the contest in Central America between Catholicism and evangelical Protestantism, it seems that the new religion of Christianity provides, especially within rural communities, only a thin veneer beneath which much of the ancient cosmology, belief and ritual continues to thrive.

THE RAIN GOD CHAC is almost everywhere at Uxmal: these heads adorn the corner of the Nunnery Quadrangle. Chac is depicted with a long, curved nose – a tapir-like proboscis, which some early Europeans interpreted as the trunk of an elephant. This schematic representation is typical of the Puuc style, from northwest Yucatán during the late Classic period (c.600–c.900).

THE MAZE OF "MAYANISM"

A Mayanist is a traditional scholar of a historical Mesoamerican civilization. Mayanism is quite different and draws upon the fringes of mainstream scholarship, being more of a collection of New Age perceptions inspired by the Pre-Columbian Mayan culture.

Several things have combined to produce Mayanism, including the end of the Long Count on 21 December 2012, the astronomical event known as galactic synchronization and the Mayan calendric prophecies. Many Maya elders and shaman-priests are dismayed by the sensationalist coverage this has provoked, which has obscured the authentic and important messages that the prophecies contain.

Mayanism combines calendar lore, prophecies, astrology, esotericism, general mysticism, mediumship and pyramidology, all loosely connected to the periphery of serious studies. Mayanism is, in fact, a maze in which it is easy to get lost while attemping to reach the centre.

THE PROPHECIES

1.

THE COMING OF FOREIGNERS AND A NEW RELIGION

During the ninth century the Maya experienced a decline in their fortunes and major sites in southern Yucatán and in the Guatemalan Highlands were abandoned. It is unclear whether the Maya had foreknowledge of this but there is no recorded prophecy to that effect. Some 400 years later, however, when their civilization was resurgent, the Maya did prophesy an invasion – the arrival of Spain's *conquistadores* in Mexico, which resulted in a disastrous cultural holocaust for the Maya.

The prophecies describe a time of "excessive sorrow . . . when the foreigners descended from the sea". The *katun*s (twenty-year cycles) on which this prophecy was based were characterized by "roguish rulers" and "harshness of face and feelings". Two important ideas are reflected in this prophecy. The first is the concept of cyclic time; in other words, that when a given *katun* period recurs, it will be accompanied by a similar pattern of events. The second is the warning of radical change.

*Ahau is the beginning of the count, because this was the **katun** when the foreigners arrived. They came from the east when they arrived. Then Christianity also began . . . The **katun** is established at Ichcaanzihoo.*

Book of Chilam Balam of Chumayel

Finally there came the great, the excessive sorrow of the sons of our wretchedness, when the foreigners descended from the sea . . . In 8 Ahau, the pueblo of the Mayapan was abandoned on account of the mountain of foreigners.

Book of Chilam Balam of Tizimin

RUINS AT TULÚM in eastern Yucatán. Chaplain Juan Díaz was the first Westerner to see the site while it was still active, reporting it as "a very large town" after making a brief coastal exploration south of Cozumel as part of Juan de Grijalva's expedition of 1518. Stephens and Catherwood later arrived there from the sea.

Anthropologists disagree about precisely what caused the ninth-century decline of Mayan civilization (see pages 16–17). Throughout history, human settlements have been affected by war or famine, but there are few parallels with the Mayan "eclipse" when many of the great complexes were abandoned and slowly reclaimed by the jungle.

SIGNS OF DECLINE

From about the eighth century onward, Mayan building and new commemorative inscriptions were confined to already established towns, which suggests that the culture was no longer expanding territorially. Another indicator was the gradual reduction of inscriptions at various sites. Stelae were no longer raised, despite the fact that these were inscribed with the *katun*-end dates which were of great calendric and ritual importance – inscriptions that were significant for recording royal genealogies and the achievements of a given dynasty. Only three sites recorded *katun*-end dates in 889CE, and the final Long Count date to be recorded – cut into a piece of jade – was the *katun*-end date twenty years later in 909CE.

Given that Mayan society was established as a series of settled city-states, deeply rooted in their various locations, what could have caused such a rapid decline, culminating in sites being left to become derelict?

The possibilities include prolonged warfare, a peasants' rebellion against the ruling classes, disease, soil erosion due to deforestation, the inability of agriculture to support a growing population, a massive natural disaster (such as floods, drought, an earthquake or a comet impact) – or, as seems most likely, a combination of some of these. There is evidence of unfavourable changes in rainfall creating an extended regional dry period. As for internal rebellion, there is no significant evidence of it. However, if there was civil strife, it is likely that during the upheaval the historical and calendric records would have been destroyed as artefacts of the ruling classes – a disaster prescient of the one, clearly prophesied by the Maya, that was perpetrated centuries later by the book-burning Bishop Landa and his team of missionaries.

CULTURAL HOLOCAUST

The legacy of Friar Diego de Landa Calderón (1524–1579), a Franciscan and the bishop of the Roman Catholic archdiocese of Yucatán, is a mixed one. As bishop he was at the forefront of efforts to convert the Maya to Christianity

THE SURVIVING CODICES

Of the Maya's once numerous codices, only three survive today – named for the cities in which they are kept – together with fragments of a fourth.

The *Madrid Codex*, housed in the Museo de América in Madrid, is the product of several scribes and is thought to have been sent to the Spanish court in the 1540s by Hernán Cortés after he acquired it near Tayasal (modern-day Flores), which in 1697 was the last Mayan city to be conquered.

The *Dresden Codex*, preserved in the state library in Dresden, Germany, is the most elaborate of the codices and a significant work of art (a replica is displayed in Guatemala City). A screen-folded codex, it was probably written just before the Conquest. Its subjects include astrological charts, records of astronomical observations (particularly the cycles of Venus, notes on eclipses and the heliacal rising of the planets) and almanacs.

The *Paris Codex* was found in 1859 in the Bibliothèque Nationale in Paris, where it had lain forgotten for an unknown period of time. It has prophecies related to *tun*s and *katun*s, and a Mayan zodiac, all of which are similar to the books of the *chilam balam*.

The *Grolier Codex* was discovered in the 1960s. Kept in a museum in Mexico, its eleven pages are fragments of a larger work but the content is ordinary.

and he oversaw *auto de fé* ceremonies for the Inquisition, at one of which – held at Mani in 1562 – thousands of Mayan images and an unknown number of codices were incinerated. Landa has a prominent place in *La Leyenda Negra*, or Black Legend – a term coined by Spanish historians to refer to the biased picture of Spain's empire painted by her rivals.

This "cultural holocaust" destroyed much of the literature and undermined the traditions of Mayan culture, and it was accompanied by physical abuse that included torture. Despite Landa's role in this, he was keen to learn about native culture and he remains the principal source of much of what we know about the post-Classic Mayan civilization. Landa's book, *Relación de las cosas de Yucatán*, is the most complete treatise on Mayan calendrics, religion

and ritual that we have, though its Christianizing gloss means it should be read with caution.

PORTENTS OF SELF-DESTRUCTION

Although no prophecy of the decline of the Maya's Classic period culture has survived (if one ever existed), the Maya – as believers in cyclic time – knew enough of their region's history to have been aware that the demise of the Olmec and Zapotec cultures provided a precedent for their own civilization's mortality.

The fullest surviving prophecy of the Spanish conquest comes from a prophet known as the Cabalchen, who was living around 1500CE. His prediction for the period of Katun 13 Ahau (1519–1539) is: "Behold, within seven score years

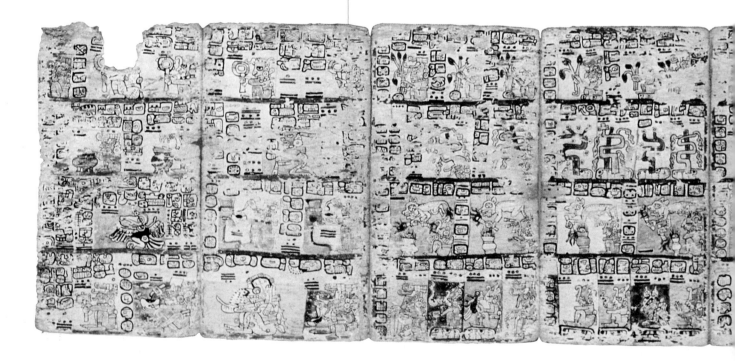

Christianity will be introduced amid the clamour of the rulers – those who violently seize the land during the *katun*." However, there exists an oral tradition of an even earlier prophecy, given in the eleventh century by Ah Xupan Naut, who predicted the coming of white men during the eighth year of Katun 13 Ahau – that is, 1527. Montejo landed on the coast of the Yucatán a year later – an astonishingly accurate prophecy over 500 years.

Because the Cabalchen's prophecy explicitly refers to Christianity it seems likely that it was "adjusted" by the Jesuits (who recorded it) to rationalize their presence and to encourage conversion. The eleventh-century prophecy leaves us in little doubt that the Maya had heard that strangers and attendant upheaval would come to the Mayan lands at a specified point in the future. (Another reading of the earlier prophecy was the return of Kukulcan (see pages 68–75.)

The Classic-period glory of the eighth-century Maya was clearly not all it seemed, if failing ecology, agriculture and inter-state rivalry are reliable signs. While the seeds of the vital staple crop of maize may have failed, the factor that contributed most virulently to the Maya's destruction may well have been self-inflicted. The Mayan prophecies suggest that our own civilization is at risk for similar reasons – another theme that threads its way through the prophecies.

THE MADRID CODEX is one of only four surviving Mayan folding books. Probably produced after the Spanish had arrived, it is a 112-page compilation of almanacs and texts thought to have been written, mostly in Yucatec, by a scribe in Tayasal, the last Mayan city to fall (in 1697).

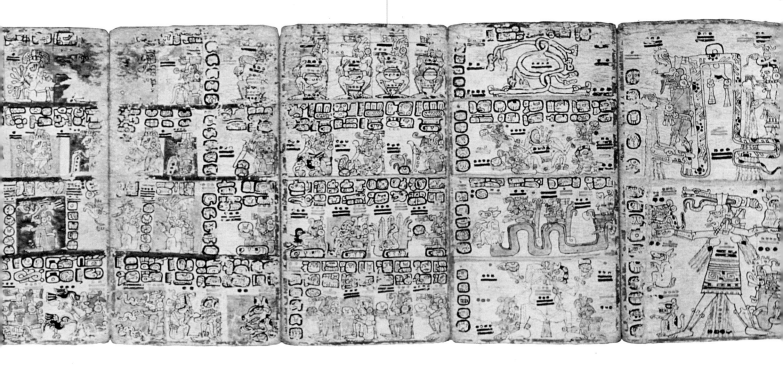

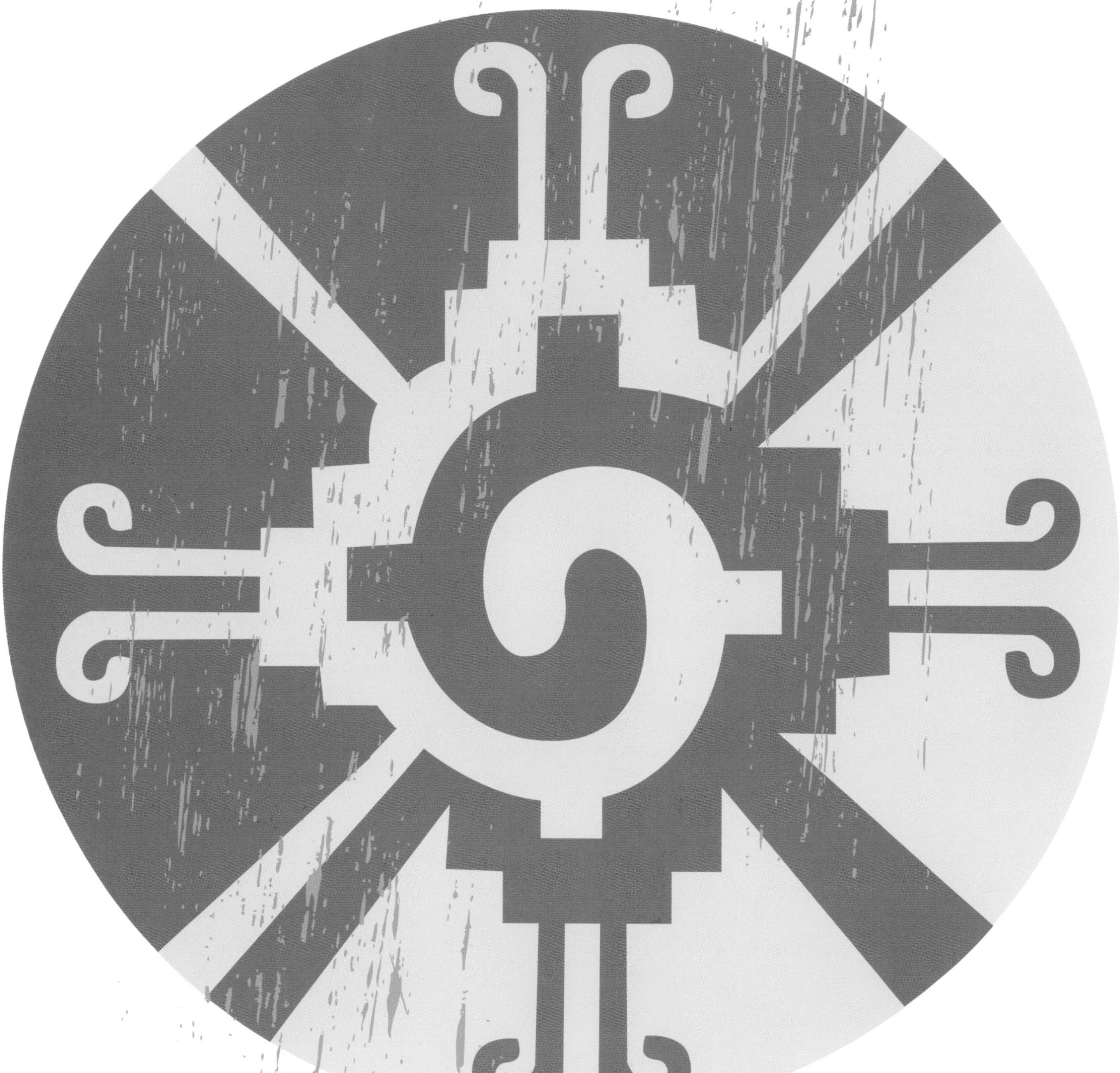

2.
EMERGENCE OF NEW MASTERS AND TEACHERS

This prophecy predicts a time when the ancient hidden wisdom will be given to the world by a new generation. The subject is the return, in the future, of initiates to the sacred land of the Maya, whose responsibility will be to show people how to experience "cosmic wisdom", thus continuing the work of the Great Spirit.

There is, however, one crucial aspect to the fulfilment of this prophecy today – the initiates will be drawn not solely from among the Maya but from people of all cultures and religions, young and old, regardless of sex, ethnicity or class. The main concern of these new masters will be to ease the problems caused by the failure of human society to meet its educational ideals and responsibilities, and to correct the extent to which the negative influences of a materialistic lifestyle, and the overuse of the planet's natural resources, have restricted our spiritual growth.

The *Popul Vuh*, the main source for Mayan creation myths, tells how the gods attempted to create human

Katun 7 Ahau is the third katun. Yaxal Chac is the face of the katun in the heavens, to its rulers, to its wise man . . . There is no great teaching. Heaven and Earth are truly lost to them; . . . Then the head-chiefs of the towns, the rulers of the towns, the prophets of the towns, the priests of the Maya are hanged. Understanding is lost; wisdom is lost.

Book of Chilam Balam of Chumayel

These masters will come from many places. They will be of many colours. Some will speak of things difficult to understand. Others will be aged. Some less so. Some will dance while others will remain silent as rocks. Their eyes will communicate the initiatic message, which is to continue through the cycles of the next millennium.

Hunbatz Men

beings from different kinds of raw material. Eventually, people were successfully made out of maize, but the gods were quick to realize that their new creation presented a challenge to their own supremacy. Consequently, they re-created humans, depriving them of knowledge and insights in order to render them less than omniscient. The result is that humans are left with a feeling that there is more to life and the universe than meets the eye.

Another myth tells how the early shamans and day-keepers first became custodians of "recovered knowledge" (hidden wisdom that went underground at the Spanish conquest, to be preserved). This responsibility was passed from family to family, the custodianship holding good through the demise of Mayan civilization during the ninth century and continuing until 1475, when there was a reunion of the Supreme Mayan Priestly Council. At the assembly it was disclosed that a period amounting to twice the 260-year *tzolkin* cycle – that is, 520 years – would elapse before "the darkness", duly brought to the Yucatán by Spain in the sixteenth century, would disperse. Thus, in 1995 Mayan solar culture was revitalized and the wisdom that had been guarded and hidden was made available to the world. Hunbatz Men presided over this "solar initiation" at the great temple complex of Chichén Itzá, an occasion that was part-fulfilment of this particular prophecy.

A CELESTIAL SERPENT intertwines a *tzolkin*-based almanac in the *Madrid Codex*. It is thought this creature may represent a rattle-tailed rain serpent associated with agricultural fertility during a period when Venus passes by the Pleiades.

THE SACRED ART OF THE BOOK

 Much of the ancient wisdom of the Maya was recorded in a type of screenfold book known as a codex, which consisted of strips of tree-bark paper prepared with a layer of limewash. The writing was in a Mesoamerican form of hieroglyphics, some examples of which date to the third century BCE.

The Mayan codices seem to have been used predominantly for divination, their content consisting of astronomical records, astrological tables, genealogies and ritual almanacs. The glyphs themselves were written in a rich and varied style; they represented both sounds in the Mayan language and whole words or concepts, drawing upon a variety of natural and abstract forms, often representing the subjects they addressed. Unlike most writing in the world, which has been developed to communicate with other people, Mayan glyphs seem to be links between earthly rulers, the gods, the cosmos and the divine – they express and are invested with a sacred nature.

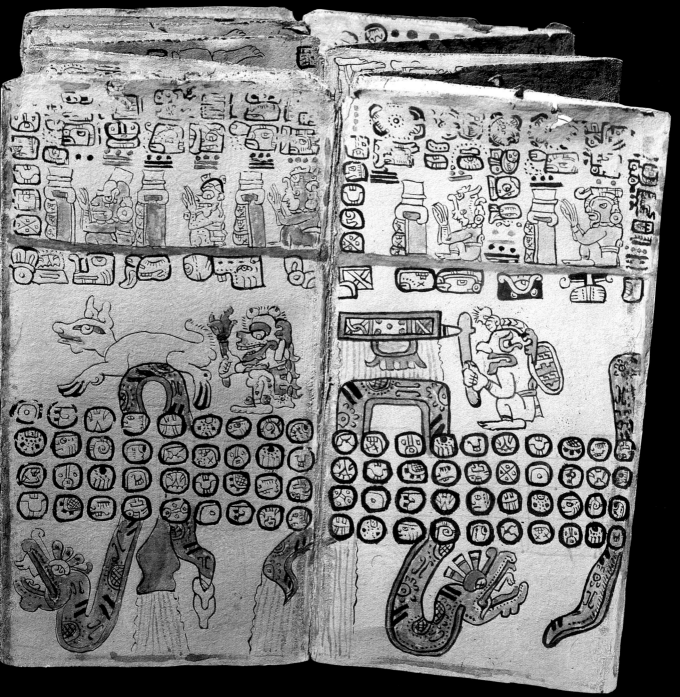

A POTENTATE IN HIS PALACE discusses matters of state with his advisors, one of them a scribe, seated in front of him at a lower level. The attendants burn tobacco in the belief that the gods might reveal themselves in the smoke.

HUNAB KU – ONE AND ALL

The event in 1995 was attended by thousands and it is sometimes referred to as the beginning of the transition from the Age of Belief to the Age of Knowledge (that is, the effects that begin to be felt during this last *katun* of the fifth sun before the cycle begins again with a new first sun). The initiation involved meditation, chanting and prayer to Hunab Ku, with the objective of reawakening the ancient knowledge of the cosmos (an "awakening" that brings to mind Buddhist notions of enlightenment). On a day of genuine spiritual experience the leaders of the Supreme Mayan Priestly Council bestowed their blessings on those gathered.

The ancient Maya were fascinated by the multifarious aspects of nature, seeing in the sky, the earth and the sea complementary elements of a vigorous and congruent whole. In the Mayan world-view, the gods, humans and mathematics are all one and the same, representing unity in plurality.

The name of the Mayan concept for the one, absolute being – the "Uncreated God" – is Hunab Ku, on whom everything is dependent. He has many epithets, including "Solitary God", "Great Hand", "Unique God" and "Giver of Movement and Measure". But if one word could sum up this abstract, incorporeal, omnipotent Mayan entity, it would probably be "energy" – a single, all-pervading energy that is understood both to have created and to support the entire observable universe, all natural phenomena and life. (For the monotheistic religions this unified energy is understood as the creator-god.)

In the Mayan languages spirit is energy, known as *kinan* – from *kin*, "the sun", and a conditional form of the verb "to be". Spirit is the sun's being, or energy. The soul is a manifestation of the spirit; it is energy endowed with intelligence, housed in a body. It is the soul that is understood as "Measure" and the spirit as "Movement". In combination, what this amounts to is form and its vitalizing energy, which provides the unifying principle. All of this is represented by the Mayan concept of Hunab Ku, who is often closely associated with the supreme creator god Itzamná (see pages 32 and 90–91).

THE AGE OF KNOWLEDGE

The Mayan prophets during the Age of Belief are known as *chilam* and they constitute a special branch of the native religion – the "jaguar priests", guardians of esoteric ancestral knowledge, thought to have descended from a shamanic priesthood.

A true shaman is not a magician, or a medicine man, although his practices may combine something of both. In a Jungian sense, a shaman is a psychopomp who serves his people by mediating between the material world and the spirit world, the realms of the conscious and the unconscious. The *chilam* was a specialist in using a state of trance during which his soul or spirit left his body, either to ascend to a heavenly domain or to descend to the Underworld. A *chilam*'s relationship with his "helping spirit" was not one of possession, but of cooperation and dialogue, whether the spirit was that of a deceased person, an animal, or an emanation of nature. It was while communicating with these spirits that the *chilam* received the prophecies.

The tradition of the *chilam* among the Maya is a variant of a phenomenon found throughout Mesoamerica, and still practised by Maya in modern-day Guatemala. Inevitably, perhaps, because of the 2012 end-date of the Mayan calendars, there is a considerable and gathering interest in what the Maya have to say, both through their ancient prophecies and in the broader teachings of the contemporary elders and shaman-teachers. Hunbatz Men, Aluna Joy Yaxk'in, Don Alejandro Oxlaj and José Argüelles figure prominently among these sages, and their work and writings have attracted a considerable following.

In his *Secrets of Mayan Science/Religion*, Mayan day-keeper Hunbatz Men explains how we can harness seven innate powers to help each of us to realize our true cosmic faculties and become Kukulcan – that is, one who knows how to transform sacred energy in our minds and bodies. Symbolically represented by the serpent and manifesting as a living presence twice a year on the pyramid at Chichén Itzá (see page 73), this cosmic power, once imbued, should be used not selfishly but for the good of all living beings.

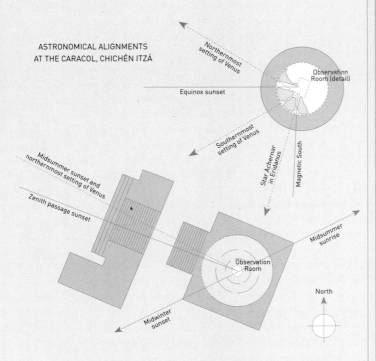

ASTRONOMICAL ALIGNMENTS
AT THE CARACOL, CHICHÉN ITZÁ

Northernmost setting of Venus

Equinox sunset

Observation Room (detail)

Southernmost setting of Venus

Star Achernar in Eridanus

Magnetic South

Midsummer sunset and northernmost setting of Venus

Zenith passage sunset

Observation Room

Midsummer sunrise

North

Midwinter sunset

3.

RESTORATION OF MAYAN CEREMONIAL SITES

Mayan temples may be reminiscent of other structures seen around the world, from the pyramids of ancient Egypt to the ziggurats of Mesopotamia, but they are actually quite distinctive. One similarity is the common inspiration, almost certainly derived from a dominant feature in nature – the mountain, which the towering pyramid temple clearly replicates. A pyramid, with its broad base, is the simplest solution to the problem presented when people in the ancient world wished to construct a building that was both tall and secure.

Apart from this shared model and certain stylistic likenesses, there is no evidence of intercontinental influence – pyramids are an example of parallel but independent development. In fact, across the Mayan territories the shape of pyramids varies widely. However, most Mayan pyramids have two core functions: they incorporate a place for worship and they serve as a funerary monument.

When the thirteenth tun arrives on his [the Year-bearer's] day and 13 Muluc falls on the first day of Pop, on the day 1 Oc there will be majesty, when Pop shall descend, when Zam shall descend in Tun 13. At the ceremonies there will be overwhelming grandeur, the impressive majesty of the heavens.

Book of Chilam Balam of Tizimin

The Mayan ceremonial centres begin to emanate the light of the new millennium which is much needed today. Many Mayan cosmic ceremonial centres begin to beckon with their solar reflection the many initiates who will come to continue the work of the Great Spirit.

Hunbatz Men

ACROPOLISES FOR THE AFTERLIFE

One of the largest Mayan sites of all is Tikal, or Tik'al. Within the six square miles (16 sq km) that have been mapped at the core of this once bustling metropolis there are approximately 3,000 buildings. These structures range from high temple-pyramids and huge palaces to small thatch-roofed huts. The pyramids are burial complexes – acropolises that dominate Tikal's sacred centre. In the late Classic period, just before the communities began to decline, the number of inhabitants may have been 90,000 or more, which makes Tikal's population density higher than that of the average modern city.

Located in the region of El Petén, where there is little permanent surface water, the site had thirteen ancient reservoirs, which would have been large enough to sustain the community during the dry winter season. Causeways connected the many buildings, which were dominated by the huge stepped pyramids surmounted by temples, their walls built up of limestone blocks.

Other complexes pivoted around single-storied palaces that were raised on platforms lower than those that support the temples. The long, narrow, high-ceilinged rooms of these palaces may have been used for ceremonies – it is possible that the royal household lived elsewhere, in less durable buildings that have not survived. The cell-like spaces opening off the corridor-like rooms have a monastic feel about them: they may have been occupied by priests.

Throughout the world, sacred architecture is used to express a culture's mythology and spiritual beliefs, with core ideas frequently reflected in a building's structural form and decoration. A sacred structure will also be intended to provide a suitably impressive theatre for performing rituals. The Maya believed that thirteen was a magical number whose patron god was Chac, the deity of fertility and life-giving rain. The number underpinned the computations used in their calendar system (see pages 22–27) – notably the thirteen *baktun*s of the Long Count – and it had cosmic significance because the Upper World was subdivided into thirteen layers, "heavens" or "skies", each presided over by a god. This is why some buildings have thirteen steps, the climbing of which is an enactment of passing through these thirteen levels.

That certain places are charged with a sense of the sacred is something with which Western culture is losing touch. Our sensitivity to "place" has been numbed by our exploitation of the planet's resources and our widespread

TIKAL'S MAIN PLAZA with Temple I (left) facing Temple II (right). In the foreground is the North Acropolis, and in the background is the Central Acropolis. Tikal rose to prominence during the Classic period and its rulers are well documented.

disregard for nature; fewer people are receptive to the numinous power and holiness of sites that were once sacred to the masses, and even in traditional places of worship perhaps only a minority have a real feeling for the "other". In a country such as India, still steeped in traditional values, the perceived sacredness of the land still gives a sense of unity to a diversity of religions, cultures and races. Wherever we live, and whatever path we follow, this prophecy calls upon us to recover our sensitivity to places charged with spiritual energy and "presence".

RECOVERY OF THE SACRED

The Maya's recovery of their most precious sites might be said to have begun with the discovery, in what is now the southernmost Mexican state of Chiapas, of Palenque (meaning "fortification"). Originally a city-state, it was at its zenith during the seventh century CE, but a century later it had declined and was finally abandoned to the jungle. In 1567 the area was visited by a Spanish priest, Pedro Lorenzo de la Nada, who wrote the first accounts of the buildings. But it was only some 200 years later, in the late eighteenth century, that a serious exploration and excavation began under Ramón de Ordoñez y Aguilar, then a little later by Antonio del Río. Further visits were made during the nineteenth century, but it was not until 1949 that a team led by Alberto Ruz Lhuillier fully recovered the site. Palenque is immensely rich in hieroglyphic inscription, carved on the monuments, temples and stelae. From these a history has been reconstructed that records the seventh-century ruling dynasty, and the rivalry between city-states that probably contributed to its downfall. Its most famous ruler was Pacal the Great, whose extraordinary tomb is in the Temple of the Inscriptions. His dates, transcribed from the Mayan calendar, were 23 March 603 to 28 August 683. (See also pages 76–83.)

AS ABOVE, SO BELOW

Other sites similarly recovered include: Ek Balam, Oxkintok, Mayapan, Chichén Itzá, Yaxchilán and Tikal. Plans of each of these sites indicate that the buildings were laid out to mirror the structure of the stellar constellations above them. It is not known how the Maya measured the movements of the stars and planets selected from among the 3,000-plus which are visible to the naked eye at any one time and location. It seems possible that buildings, or features of buildings, may have served as sight-lines. Astronomer Anthony Aveni and architect Horst Hartung have determined that the ancient Maya used architecture, and specifically doorways and windows, for astronomical sightings, especially of Venus (see diagram, page 63). Certainly, some of the buildings on each major site are aligned with the positions of bodies such as the sun, moon or Venus, or a constellation or star-cluster.

There is no astronomy without advanced mathematics, and the three points of the rising, zenith and setting of a

EL CARACOL at Chichén Itzá was given its nickname of "the Snail" by the Spanish because of its round summit and the spiral staircase used to access it. The structure is actually an observatory, carefully configured so that certain astronomical alignments could be monitored (see diagram, page 63).

heavenly body provided the triangle that was one of the basic features of Mayan geometry calculations.

Tikal provides an example of how the combination of a building's location, its structure and carefully placed stelae, provide an alignment from which it is possible to plot the movements of stars and planets from a given position. At Uaxactun, in Guatemala, the so-called Group E buildings map the motions of the sun over the course of a year. The rising sun is viewed from the central pyramid, and the alignment is made by means of three temples representing four particular days. The northern temple, by means of windows or doors, aligns with the rising sun of the summer solstice; the southern temple with the winter solstice; and the middle temple with the two equinoxes when the length of the day is equal to the length of the night. Probably the most famous example of astro-architecture is El Caracol at Chichén Itzá (see diagram, page 63). The building's staircase is set at 27.5 degrees north of west, which makes it perfectly aligned to mark the most northerly position of Venus. The northeast and southwest corners of the building form a diagonal that aligns with the summer solstice sunrise and the winter solstice sunset. The window shafts in the round tower align with other significant astronomical events.

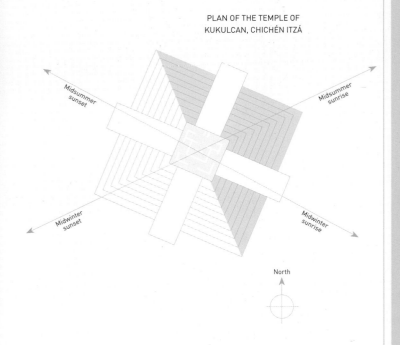

PLAN OF THE TEMPLE OF
KUKULCAN, CHICHÉN ITZÁ

Midsummer sunset

Midsummer sunrise

Midwinter sunset

Midwinter sunrise

North

THE RETURN OF A SUPREME BEING

Would that he might return from the west, uniting us in commiseration over our present unhappy plight! This is the fulfilment of the prophecies of Katun 5 Ahau. . . . God grant that there may come a Deliverer from our afflictions, who will answer our prayers in Katun 1 Ahau!

Book of Chilam Balam of Tizimin

The prophecy of the return of a supreme being is a theme in all the major religions, though it may not appeal greatly to the secular mind. The supreme being of whom Prophecy 4 speaks is Quetzalcoatl, a Toltec (and, later, Aztec) deity who was adopted by the Maya during the Post-Classic era, when peoples from northern Mexico began to move into territories further south once the Mayan city-states had weakened. Quetzalcoatl is a highly influential deity in Mesoamerican mythology and the Maya knew him as Kukulcan (*kukul* "feathered", *can* "serpent"). He was associated with the west, the direction of the setting sun, darkness and death. His emblem was the plumed serpent, and among the Maya his associated colour was black. His cult was prominently represented at those Mayan sites in Yucatán where the militarized Toltec influence was felt most strongly, such as Chichén Itzá (see box, page 73) and Mayapan. The prophecy of his return subsequently became central to Mayan belief.

The "return", and what is meant by it, is understood to be imminent because the *katun* prophecy that speaks most clearly of the return of this supreme being is that of Katun 4 Ahau, the current era which terminates the Long Count calendar at the winter equinox in 2012. The *Book of Chilam Balam of Chumayel* prophesies as follows:

"The *katun* is established at Chichén Itzá. The settlement of the Itzá shall take place [there]. The quetzal shall come, the green bird shall come. Ah Kantenal shall come. Blood-vomit shall come. Kukulcan shall come with them for the second time. [It is] the word of God."

We do not know who or what Kantenal is, unless it is a variant rendering of Kukulcan. "Blood-vomit" may be a reference to yellow fever, which could mean an actual epidemic of that virus, or perhaps it alludes metaphorically to the "disease" represented by the Spanish invasion. It might have been both. The most significant point, however, is that Kukulcan is expected to make his reappearance when the world is most in need of him – a belief that is

THE TEMPLE OF KUKULCAN at Chichén Itzá is a step-pyramid that dates to between the 10th and 13th centuries. It has 365 steps in total, one for each day of the *haab*, and it is carefully aligned (see diagram, page 69, and box, page 73).

THE QUETZAL-FEATHERED SERPENT

The Mesoamerican god Quetzalcoatl was not worshipped by the Maya in the Classic period: his cult was imported into the Mayan territories by Toltec invaders from the north. It is thought that the Quetzal-Feathered Serpent (*coatl* refers to the rattlesnake) was originally a culture hero who had introduced civilization to Tula, the Toltec capital, but had then been defeated by his evil twin brother (*coatl* also means "twin", a pairing motif that is matched in the Mayan Hero Twins),

whereupon he retreated to the coast but promised to return one day. At the shore he was transformed into a feathered serpent with a flaming tail, ascended into the sky and became Venus. Not merely a god, he was also an ancestor figure.

Images of a plumed serpent were first made among the Olmecs, around 1000BCE, and the earliest appearance of the quetzal serpent is a carving at the Temple of Quetzalcoatl at Teotihuacán, dated to the third century CE. This

miraculous synthesis of bird and serpent is a reptile clothed in what are said to be the most precious of all feathers – the iridescent blue-green and scarlet tail plumage of the quetzal bird.

During his evolution, Kukulcan has been variously thought of as a deity of water, the god of abundance and fertility, and the god of the rain-bringing clouds – that is, weather in its life-giving aspect.

consistent with the "messianic" hopes of other religions throughout the world.

This belief in the return of Quetzalcoatl–Kukulcan was so deeply embedded in the Mesoamerican mind that, in a historical twist of fate for the peoples of the region, when Cortés presented himself to the Aztec ruler Moctezuma II (reigned 1502–1520) in November 1519, he was greeted with the words: "My royal ancestors have said that you would come to visit your city and that you would sit upon your mat and chair when you returned."

As cited in the *Book of Chilam Balam of Chumayel*, myths dating back centuries proclaim the future reappearance of Quetzalcoatl–Kukulcan. These myths relate how he vows to return, conquer his enemies and establish a new dominion of piety and good government. The message of brotherly love and the story of Christ's death and resurrection preached by the Spanish missionaries fortuitously enabled the newcomers to make use of the long-held belief in Kukulcan's return to attract converts to Christianity. As the anthropologist Alfred Tozzer explained, "these prophecies were doubtless adapted by the Spanish to proselytizing purposes, but they seem fundamentally to have been native accounts of the return of Kukulcan."

SOLUTIONS LIE WITHIN

As far as the Maya are concerned, this prophecy does not need to be interpreted literally as a reincarnation of Kukulcan. Rather, the hope lies in the themes of Prophecy 12 and Prophecy 13 (see pages 122–129) – that is, through enlightenment and the transformation of consciousness. By means of their own spiritual evolution, ordinary people will develop the character and attributes of the supreme being. By the "initiation of cosmic wisdom . . . people can attain the same, high spiritual state, so as to 'become' Kukulcan . . . We need only develop our faculties of consciousness to fully realize that status." The prophecy can therefore be viewed as one about the recovery of an energy drawn from the Earth and creatively transformed to resolve the problems we face as we approach 2012.

In the prophecies of the return recorded in the *chilam balam* books different names are used for the deity in question. The accounts suggest a gradual transition from the variously named gods of the Maya to the one god, Hunab Ku. The resurgence of Mayan civilization and culture, after its sudden Post-Classic decline, has been aided by this movement toward monotheism – the one god being a reflection of the one, united people.

The world's major religions also expect the return of a Supreme Being, Teacher or Saviour at a time in the future when humankind is at risk. The Messiah of Judaism will come to bring the scattered Children of Israel together, finally ensuring peace in the Middle East; the Second Coming of Christ will initiate the Day of Judgment and the inauguration of paradise; alongside him will be the Mahdi, the redeemer of Islam; similarly, Hinduism looks to Kalki, and Buddhism to Maitreya. Each forms a part of the

CHICHÉN ITZÁ AND THE ANIMATED EQUINOX

The prophecy that speaks of the return of a supreme being – the prophecy of Katun 4 Ahau – was established at Chichén Itzá. Historical sources tell the story of a man, called Kukulcan, who arrived from the west during Katun 4 Ahau (ending in 987CE). The history is confused as to whether there was a conquest of the Toltec state of Chichén, or whether a people called the Itzá moved into Yucatán during a later Katun 4 Ahau. Either way, it seems that from the earliest times images of Kukulcan as the plumed serpent have been of great significance at Chichén Itzá, and that from this great royal capital the imagery spread across many Mayan city-states.

The name Chichén Itzá means "Opening of the Wells of the Itzá", a reference to two limestone sinkholes, or cenotes, that provided fresh water in this largely riverless region (see page 12). The larger of the two is the Sacred Cenote, revered by the local Maya and so called because of the belief that the life-giving rain deity was present there. A ceremonial pathway, or sak be, links the principal site to the Sacred Cenote, which the Spanish subsequently came to know as the Well of Sacrifice. The cenote was just one part of the larger complex where victims were offered to the gods as part of sacrificial rituals.

At the sacred heart of Chichén Itzá stood El Castillo, or the Temple of Kukulcan. This four-sided temple-mountain has a stairway running up each of its sides and it serves as a monumental sundial – the axis that runs through the northeast and southwest corners of the structure is oriented toward the rising sun at the summer solstice and the setting sun at the winter solstice (see diagram, page 69). Each stairway has an enormous balustrade in the form of a feathered serpent, its mouth agape at the bottom (see illustration, page 71). The position of the main doorway signifies that the northern stairway of the temple is the principal one out of the four, and this is confirmed twice a year at the time of the spring and autumn equinoxes. On those evenings the steps of the pyramid cast shadows across the northeast balustrade wall, appearing to make the rattlesnake sculpture come to life with diamond-back patterning.

Snake motifs are repeated at the Temple of the Warriors, where two fearsome-looking feathered Vision Serpents form the door columns and symbolize the animal's role of shamanic helper, aiding the living to communicate with the afterlife (see page 75).

As with peoples elsewhere in the world, the Maya were fascinated by the fact that snakes swallowed their prey and shed their skins. This behaviour supported the idea that serpents were the means of rebirth and renewal. The jaguar, the caiman and the bird of prey were all accorded powerful meaning by the Maya, but the snake was used most widely in their religious symbolism.

religion's eschatology – that is, its doctrine of the final events or ultimate destiny of humankind. For the Maya, hope resides in their traditional wisdom and its teaching, with all of humankind learning the lessons of the Maya's mistakes and "coming of age" to assume responsibility for our relationships and the well-being of our planet.

THE ENERGY-TRANSFORMING SNAKE

This prophecy has a dimension that lies beyond the myth, since it speaks of a resurgence of the kind of energy that is associated with *kundalini* meditation – derived from releasing the dormant energy of the coiled serpent sleeping at the bottom of the spine. This can be understood as an energy that transforms people: in snake-like fashion, human beings will slough off their old "skins", leaving behind a materialistic way of life. It is the quetzal part of the plumed serpent that inspires the mind to take flight, thus gaining new perceptions. Nations evolve just as individuals do, and the plumed serpent mythology of the Maya represents a particular period in the growth and development of Mayan culture.

Out of the diverse pantheon of Mayan gods, from one region of the Mayan realm Kukulcan began his emergence as their one, true god. In the books of the *chilam balam*

ROYAL WOMEN AT BONAMPAK pierce their tongues with a stingray spine then pull through a rope, which has thorns or obsidian flakes attached. A shark's tooth was another popular "perforator". Such bloodletting acts were often held in public, on a platform in the open plaza. This computer-aided reconstruction is from an ancient Mayan mural at Bonampak, Room 3.

various passages foretell how once separate deities will gradually become one, regardless of the names used. In Mayan history this remains an unrealized ideal.

The snake's primal, slithery movement, as well as its phallic associations, meant that it was incorporated into many Mayan ritual dances that were expressive of states of ecstasy. Both the priests and the lords of the city-states danced with live snakes, and through such ritual the king could create a doorway to the spiritual world and attain power to effect beneficial change.

However, by far the strongest associations with snakes were in the form of vision rites used to summon the Vision Serpent, which provided a channel between the natural and supernatural realms, enabling members of the elite to commune with their ancestors and the gods. These rituals consisted of auto-sacrificial bloodletting to induce a trance-like state. Blood was let from a soft body part and sprinkled onto paper, mixed with other materials and burned to produce a cloud of incense.

Usually depicted as a rearing snake, sometimes partially flayed and often wearing feathered fans, the Vision Serpent commonly has blood attached to its tail to symbolize the substance from which it materialized. When called up by the rite, the ancestral dead and the divinities could leave Xibalba and be conveyed into the world of the living. Over time, at Chichén Itzá (see box, page 73) feathered serpent imagery in the form of Kukulcan became more identified with the divinity of the state than a reference to the means by which individual kings once communicated with the founders of their lineages.

5.
PACAL VOTAN – THE MAGICIAN OF TIME

"

As the special witness of time, I, Pacal Votan, know the perfect count of days. I bow in the temple of the tower and the rock, the sanctuary of Bolon Ik. In my body, formed of the ultimate perfection of God's power of all movement and measure (Hunab Ku), is the recollection that is prophecy.

Pacal Votan

"

King Pacal Votan (603–683CE) is perhaps the most famous ruler of the city-state of Palenque. He ascended to the throne when he was around twelve years old and therefore reigned for about sixty-eight years. Pacal's full name is Kinich Janaab Pacal, or "Sun Shield", and he was responsible for a programme of building that includes some of the finest examples of Mayan art and architecture. Because of the inscriptions carved onto these monuments, which record precise astronomical and astrological information, Pacal is also known as "the Magician of Time" or "Time's Special Witness". Another variant on the name of this seventh-century prophet-king is Pacal Votan, which means "Closer of the Cycle" – that is, the closer of the great cycle of time that concludes with the winter solstice on 21 December 2012. His prophecies are of particular interest, having been delivered post-mortem from his concealed tomb in the Temple of Inscriptions at Palenque.

Pacal's prophecies (preserved orally by the priests) were thought to have been communicated via a telektonon (see box, below) through a system of numbers. His epigram "All is number – God is number – God is in all" links with Hunab Ku, the "Giver of Movement and Measure". The two concepts bind to suggest that mathematics, together with movement and measure, is the source of life. Balance, order and harmony combine as the expression of both the spiritual and physical life of the cosmos. This prophecy calls us to use personal, collective and cosmic energy to transcend the materialism and technological dominance of our age, to address the ecological crisis, and to prepare for what, in all likelihood, will be a problematic transition into the next world age.

Pacal's prophecies are warnings not of catastrophe but of spiritual evolution. His prophetic vision was "that humanity as a species would become disconnected from the laws of the natural world and would fall ignorant of our sacred interdependence with nature".

Pacal was deified at his death (see box, below) and after being interred in his hidden tomb in the Temple of

KING PACAL was buried with this magnificent jade funerary mask and jewelry. Jade was the most favoured material among the Mayan nobility. Pacal's grave goods make it clear that he intended to increase his prestige in the netherworld.

THE TALKING STONE OF PROPHECY

Alberto Ruz Lhuillier, the Mexican archaeologist working at Palenque in 1948, noticed a large panel in the floor of the upper room in the Temple of Inscriptions. The filled holes along one edge suggested that it was a trap-door. So began a tale of discovery – of the tomb of Pacal Votan, celebrated for its ornate sarcophagus cover, representing Pacal's fall down the great trunk of the World Tree and into the open jaws of the otherworld. Lhuillier later uncovered a stone "spirit" tube that ran from the burial chamber to the head of the Vision Serpent in the temple above, enabling the deceased to function as a kind of oracle, transmitting his prophecies to any priests who came to consult a ruler deified at his death and worshipped as a god.

The design on this sarcophagus cover inspired theories that the Maya were influenced by extraterrestrial life. Erich von Däniken's *Chariots of the Gods* (1968) was the first of several books that proposed the "astronaut theory" – the idea that it was aliens who gave the Maya their knowledge of mathematics, astronomy and the cyclic concept of time. Däniken claimed that the image of the king suggested the position of an astronaut lying in a space-capsule at take-off.

Inscriptions, priests visited to consult him as an oracle. The message he transmitted was that a knowledge of astronomy and mathematics would enable the Maya to create their calendars, which in turn provided them with the means to produce their prophecies.

Pacal personified the Mayan holistic understanding of the spirit, the soul, the gods, human beings and numbers, or mathematics. It is from the subtle integration of all these that Mayan calendars were constructed and the energies for prophecy sourced. The sacredness of numbers to the Maya is based on the belief that numbers are the key to the real, underlying structure of the universe – a thesis that modern quantum mechanics and number theory seem to be supporting.

THE GLORIOUS LEGACY OF PACAL

If an appreciation of the importance of mathematics in seeking to understand the workings of the cosmos was a significant intellectual legacy to leave to the people of Palenque, Pacal's material and political achievements during a long reign were even more remarkable. During his lifetime the city-state of Palenque had survived one of the darkest periods of its history but it was transformed under his kingship into a powerful and vibrant kingdom, despite being smaller than a rival such as Tikal.

Today, Palenque's ruins, with their magnificent and exemplary courtly art and architecture, lie nestled in the foothills of the Tumbala mountains of Chiapas, Mexico, surrounded by waterfalls and beneath a deep canopy of

THE POWER OF EIGHT AND THE LIFE-GIVING MAIZE GOD

In the performance of rituals, the Mayan kings dressed as gods, or as animals believed to have divine power. By means of trances and dancing they assumed their identities and spiritual powers.

The *Popul Vuh*, the Mayan creation myth, shows that one of the most important deities was the god of maize, which represented the vital force, the

energy behind all creation – life or the breath of life itself. The king would have assumed the "form" and creative attributes of Yum Kaax, as the god was known, shown in images as both male and female, as foliated or tonsured. The foliated form denotes the number eight, and the tonsured form is linked to the start date of the Long Count. The

tonsured form is also associated with the lunar crescent and the glyphs of the lunar cycles.

The symbolism of maize extends to everyday life. The crop was the staple of the economy. Its abundance, for which the king would have accepted responsibility, was therefore essential.

THE **ENTHRONEMENT** of Palenque's King Ahkal Monabh III (left), assisted by nobles, in 9 Ik 5 Kayab, or 3 January 722ᴄᴇ. Born in 678, Ahkal sought to emulate Pacal and embarked upon a programme of construction that rivalled that of his predecessor – this relief is from the throne of Ahkal's Temple XIX at Palenque.

rainforest. Below this site stretches the verdant floodplain of the Usumacinta river. The idyllic modern atmosphere could not be more different from the scenes that must have been witnessed as the city clung precariously to its independence during the early years of Pacal's reign, when his mother probably acted as regent.

By about 650 the situation appears to have been stabilized and Pacal was able to consolidate his power and realize his vision for a city-state. All the while, war continued against Calakmul and its allies, especially around the frontiers to the east and northeast. Despite these campaigns, wealth accumulated from well-managed agriculture, and the control of regional trade routes, enabled Pacal to begin transforming the city through a generously funded building campaign.

Pacal Votan's architecture was inventive: the weightiness typical of structures seen elsewhere was minimized by the use of dividing walls that reduced the stress on the load-bearing walls. This, in turn, permitted the development of interiors that were lighter and more airy than elsewhere in Mesoamerica. Although few remain today, brightly painted white plaster reliefs once adorned the exteriors of many of the structures, depicting the city's succession of rulers, nobles and their families. At Palenque careful use was made of genealogical art to emphasize dynastic legitimacy. The work that Pacal

MIGHTY PALENQUE reflected its wealth and power in its buildings. Here, in the foreground, are the great palace (left) and the Temple of the Inscriptions (right). In the background (top left) is the site's ceremonial compound: the Cross Group of step-pyramid temple buildings, consisting of the Temple of the Cross (top, left), Temple of the Foliated Cross (top, centre) and Temple of the Sun (top, right).

initiated was seen to completion by two of his sons and successors, Chan-Bahlum (reigned 684–702) and Kan Hoy (c.702–720).

The city's most important buildings were the palace (its square tower is unique in the region), the Temple of the Count (so called after a Count de Waldek who camped at the site in 1831 and recorded it in a series of drawings) and the Temple of Inscriptions. The various structures that form parts of the palace complex seem to have been dedicated by Pacal between 654 and 683. However, his crowning monument, architecturally at least, was the Temple of the Inscriptions, which served as his funerary monument. It was built toward the end of his reign with many of the details completed later by Chan-Bahlum. It was in the Temple of the Inscriptions in the early 1950s that one of *the* great finds of Mayan archaeology was made: the final resting place of Pacal himself, within a magnificent limestone sarcophagus (see box, page 79).

While the Temple of the Inscriptions is rightly famous for housing the tomb of Lord Pacal, its name is actually taken from three hieroglyphic tablets positioned on the inner walls of the temple, known respectively as the East, Central and West tablets. These tablets hold 617 glyphs, comprising the second-longest Mayan inscription known to us. Often esoteric in meaning, the hieroglyphics take up a familiar theme – shared with the books of *chilam balam* – that is important for our understanding of the Mayan prophecies: the idea an event that took place in the past will recur when the *katun* recycles.

THE FAMILY IMMORTAL

After Pacal's death, Chan-Bahlum ordered the construction of a group of three pyramid temples known as the Temple of the Cross, the Temple of the Foliated Cross and the Temple of the Sun, which lie to the southeast of the palace. These are among the most elegant of all Mayan temples, echoing the shapes of mountains in the distance.

Each temple stands on its own raised base and is reached by a frontal stairway. Like the traditional Mayan home, the internal layout consists of a front and a back room. The inner sanctum is in the back room with a three-part panel, depicting the king, Chan-Bahlum, on one side as a boy, and on the other as a man. The glyphs confirm his genealogy as the rightful heir and ruler of Palenque.

Mayan kingship clearly attached great significance to lineage. The preferred pattern of succession during the Classic period was from father to oldest son, but a brother could succeed a brother, or a nephew his uncle; even a woman could succeed. In fact, Pacal's own royal claims were through his mother Ix Sak Kuk rather than his father Kan Mo Hix. The reason for this may have been that Palenque was under serious and sustained attack – its enemy believed to be the powerful kingdom of Calakmul – during Pacal's boyhood, and he may have been the strongest claimant to the throne still alive afterward. It is believed that three or four other royal candidates died within a period of eight years during Pacal's infancy.

All official genealogy authenticated the pedigree, and thereby strengthened the authority, of the incumbent ruler. Two things were needed: a clear statement of parentage, illustrating wider relationships, and a list of the birth dates for successive rulers. In the genealogies of most Mayan sites, evidence of these two conditions having been met is not often found. However, at Palenque there are several forms of "king-list", providing dates that can be checked against each other, as well as clear parentage information. When all that information is brought together, alongside other specific references to certain brothers, grandchildren, designated heirs and so on, it becomes possible to reconstruct a highly informative royal genealogy of a dozen generations for Palenque, extending over 400 years.

By consolidating his rule, establishing one of the strongest of Mayan dynasties and expanding the regional power of Palenque, "Time's Special Witness" almost certainly believed that he had created the conditions to perpetuate his own family lineage for eternity.

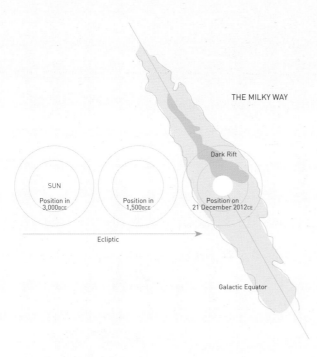

THE MILKY WAY

Dark Rift

SUN

Position in
3,000BCE

Position in
1,500BCE

Position on
21 December 2012CE

Ecliptic

Galactic Equator

6.
GALACTIC SYNCHRONIZATION

Then comes another law also in 4 Khan, the time of movement and noise in the sky, movement and noise on Earth. The sun and the Earth shall come together within the district, the navel, of the katun.

Book of Chilam Balam of Tizimin

All moons, all years, all days, all winds, reach their completion. Measured is the time in which we can know the benevolence of the sun. Measured is the time in which the stars look down on us.

Popul Vuh

This prophecy refers to a conjunction that takes place approximately every 26,000 years, an event that will next occur at the winter solstice in December 2012 – it is called "galactic synchronization". (The Maya calculated this cycle to be 25,630 years, based on five 5,126-year world ages: see page 112.) At sunrise on 21 December 2012 the solstice sun will align with the equator of our galaxy, the Milky Way, where the Earth is located. That is, the sun's rays – on the darkest day of the year – will strike within the central bulge of the saucer-shaped Milky Way, just below what is known as the "Dark Rift", at the galactic core where it is believed there is a black hole.

This alignment occurs because of a phenomenon called the precession of the equinoxes (see box, page 86), which is caused by the gravitational forces exerted on the Earth by the sun, the moon and the other planets. This prophecy tells us that the galactic synchronization marks the end of one world age and the birth of a new one.

THE EFFECT OF PRECESSION

The Earth's "precession of the equinoxes" cycle takes nearly 26,000 years. Precession is the consequence of the Earth wobbling imperceptibly at the same time as it turns on its axis during the twenty-four-hour orbit around the sun. This movement slowly shifts the apparent position of the sun relative to the backdrop of stars (at times such as a solstice, for example) by about one degree every 72 years. This means that the heavens are seen from a steadily changing point of view. For example, if a constellation were viewed through a Mayan temple window at a certain moment in the past, because of the way that the Earth moves on its axis nearly 26,000 years will elapse before that constellation completes a cycle and is returned to the place in the sky where it can be seen from that original viewpoint.

Astronomers know this change as "precession" and modern technology confirms the precession period to be 25,800 years. The Maya may have become aware of precession in the first millennium BCE. A micro-cycle (every twenty-four years) of precession was celebrated as 11 Pik. Having derived a value for precession's angular rate, the Maya were able to calculate forward to determine when the sun would conjunct with the galactic equator. The Long Count was then established to synchronize with that conjunction.

The end of the precessional cycle of 26,000 years that returns the galaxy to alignment is not a prophecy of the Maya so much as an astronomical event that, remarkably, was calculated and plotted in the Mayan calendars. The prophecy is to be found in how they interpreted the event of galactic synchronization. As John Major Jenkins has put it: "The Maya understood that whereas the 260-day sacred cycle is our period of individual gestation, the 26,000-year cycle is our collective gestation – our collective unfolding as a species."

An "unfolding" suggests a prospect of evolution, perhaps the further development of our mental, emotional and intuitive faculties. We are (modern instruments tell us) 26,000 light years away from the galactic centre, which means that the light, or energy, reaching us now began its journey toward us during the last era in which the sun at the December solstice conjuncted with the galactic centre in approximately 24,000 BCE. We can only wonder what this strange coincidence might mean.

THE PALACE OF THE MASKS at Kabah, Yucatán. Built c.800 CE, the outside wall is covered with mosaic masks of the rain god Chac: 260 in total, one for each day of the *tzolkin* calendar. There is also a frieze that contains zigzag serpents, the creature that was a portal to another cosmic level. These decorative motifs affirm the relationship between the Mayan calendars, nature and the cosmos.

7.
THE MILKY WAY PROPHECIES

The ceiba tree of abundance is their arbour . . .
the first tree of the world was rooted fast.

Book of Chilam Balam of Chumayel

The prophecies about the Milky Way combine Mayan astronomy and mythology. Astronomical observations told the Maya that the brightest part of the Milky Way was between Scorpio and Sagittarius, where the galactic centre is to be found (see also page 85). In Mayan mythology the Milky Way was the ceiba tree, which the *Book of Chilam Balam of Chumayel* describes as "the first tree of the world" – a Mayan Tree of Life, the origin of the entire planet and everything that is dependent on it both physically and spiritually. These associations with inception meant that the Maya also thought of the Milky Way as a cosmic umbilical cord and mother. The tree-image symbolism speaks of continued evolution, and the creative sustaining of life in all its forms.

The shadowy track running down the middle of the Milky Way is the "Dark Rift" – or the "dark road" to the Underworld of Xibalba, as it was called by the Quiché Maya. In myth Xibalba has several identities, such as the entrance to a cave or tunnel, the crater of a volcano, the mouth of a monster or an animal such as the jaguar, a cleft in the Cosmic Tree itself, and the birth canal of the Cosmic Mother. It is also imagined as a snake, with the Pleiades forming the rattle of its tail. The dark, womb-like centre is where the December solstice sun crosses the Milky Way, an image of the sexual union of the First Father with the First Mother. This union, achieved every 26,000-year precessional cycle, reinforces the concept of rebirth.

The Maya observed the stars of the Milky Way to predict change (such as the onset of the rainy and dry seasons). Building on the idea that the eventual alignment, or galactic synchronization, would take place at the end of the thirteenth *baktun* of the current cycle, this Milky Way prophecy anticipates more far-reaching change – a major point of transition in the Earth's history, with the commencement of a new world age and an unprecedented creative shift in human consciousness and civilization.

MAYAN COSMOLOGY

The Milky Way forms only a part of the Mayan concept of the universe, which is that of a stratified entity made up of several interconnected parts: a square, earthly realm bounded by two supernatural ones: above is the sky, the Upper World, and below is Xibalba, the fearsome Underworld.

Each of these realms had a complement of deities. At the centre, providing the link between them, was the World Tree, the cosmic ceiba. Some accounts state that the sky had thirteen layers, while Xibalba had nine. The sky was supported by four other ceiba trees, one at each corner. These four cardinal points were the *bacab*, sons of Hunab Ku. The date of creation was calculated to have been 13.0.0.0.0 4 Ahau 8 Cumku, which equates to 13 August 3114BCE – and at around this time each year Orion rises in the sky near the point at which the Milky Way crosses the ecliptic, reaching its highest point in the sky just before dawn. The creative cycle of the cosmos was perceptible.

The cardinal directions and the *bacab* trees each had a colour associated with them. The sky has six of its thirteen stepped levels rising to the eastern horizon, which is red because of the path of the sun rising to its zenith. In astronomy, east was identified with Venus as the Morning Star. Red symbolized vital forces – from the divine element of blood to fire and the sap of the sacred ceiba tree.

One step rises to the top, the highest celestial level where the creator god Itzamná lives. In imitation of the mythology associated with Itzamná's abode, the temple of many pyramid structures is located on a one-step upper platform. A deity with many manifestations, Itzamná is sometimes identified as Hunab Ku. In the New Year rituals he dresses as a high priest, in which mode he invented the priestly art of writing (see page 20). The significance of his name is

THE MILKY WAY was believed by the Maya to be the path taken by souls on their journey between the Upper World (the sky, or *caan*) and Xibalba, the Underworld domain of the dead.

vague: it might be derived from the word for "caiman" (*itzam*), or it might refer to rain, or dew.

Six steps descend to the western horizon, which is black because it is the path of the declining sun. The west was associated with the kingdom of the dead, and darkness – a time of divination when one could contact the gods.

Xibalba lies below the horizon, and this dread place has nine levels. Four descend to the nadir, a single step represents the descent down to the lowest level, and four rise back to the surface.

The Yucatec word for south, *nolh*, means "the sun's large side" and it bears the colour yellow, reminiscent of the solar disc and ripening maize, which expressed abundance and life itself.

The north is *xaman*, for the tropics-dwelling Maya the most distant cardinal point. It referred to "the sun's left side" or "the place next to paradise", and its colour is white (*sak*), a positive hue and the symbol of royalty and purity. The Milky Way was *sak be*, or the "white road". The North Star is the unmoving pivot of the universe.

FATES WRITTEN IN THE COSMOS

There are several sources for Mayan astrology, including the *Dresden Codex*, which provides data on the 584-day cycle of Venus, an important calendar for Mayan astrologers, who calculated with great precision the dates of the planet's transit across the face of the sun. This information was used to cast individual horoscopes, although most astrologers were more concerned with what planetary conjunctions might signify for their local communities.

Periods of time, such as the twenty-year *katun*, are marked with characteristics. As with individuals, a *katun* is expected to "behave" according to those characteristics.

The Earth itself is a subject for astrological analysis, based not on a birth date, but on its alignments with other planets at any given time. In interpreting the character of recurring periods of time and transposing that reading into prophecies, what the Maya were doing was reading the Earth's horoscope. They seemed to understand that astrology was concerned with archetypes – that behind every form there is an original model, or template, the dynamic of which influences human character and experience. The power of such archetypes goes beyond mere prediction. The Maya were putting together a diagnosis of the Earth based on conjunctions that occur with the solstices and equinoxes across nearly 26,000 years, through to the next galactic synchronization due in 2012.

The third cosmic world, the earthly realm centred between the upper and lower worlds, where mortals lived, had the colours blue and green (*yax*, the one word used for both). Blue-green was closely linked to the life-giving element of water, treasured in its stone forms of turquoise and jade. Blue-green was also the predominant colour during the rites of sacrifice.

NATURAL AND SUPERNATURAL

To understand Mayan cosmology and how life itself was regarded, it is useful to reflect on what Westerners believe to be the nature of reality. In the Western mind "real" things are objects or facts, and a sharp distinction is made between the "real" (the natural) and the "supernatural". The Maya did not think in this way. Everything, be it an object, a name, an idea, a fact or an event, had both natural and supernatural aspects. A king could be a deity and a mythological deity could be human, and neither was omnipotent nor omniscient: they could be killed and brought back to life. Trees, minerals, rocks, water and crops (especially maize) could be both utilitarian and embody supernatural energy and significance. In the Mayan creation story human beings were made out of maize (see page 95) in a way that recalls the Genesis story of God creating Adam out of earth.

THE KING OF COPÁN depicted on the city's Stela B wears a neck-bar that is emitting two Chacs, possibly because at the moment of the date on the stela Venus was at its maximum elongation in an area of the sky that corresponds to our constellation Virgo, which the Maya associated with Chac.

The principal source of Mayan creation mythology is the *Popul Vuh* (*Book of the Community*), a sacred manuscript of the Quiché Maya people preserved for posterity by elders in the wake of the Spanish conquest. Containing a mixture of myth and history, the work has three parts: the creation of the Earth and attempts to make its first inhabitants; the legend of the Hero Twins and their antecedents; and the successful creation of humans, including the founding of the Quiché dynasties.

The creative work began with the search for the right ingredients. Animals assisted the creator gods by finding a location where there were useful plants and fruits, including cacao and plums – but most important of all were the white and yellow strains of maize. The animals gathered the maize and took it to Xmucane, who ground it and mixed it with water to form a dough. The two creator gods Heart of Sky and Sovereign Plumed Serpent then moulded the first people, known as "mother-fathers".

The *Popul Vuh* describes the earlier act of the creation of the Earth in similar terms to a farmer's measurement and preparation of a four-sided maize field:

"the fourfold siding, fourfold cornering,
measuring, fourfold staking,
halving the cord, stretching the cord
in the sky, on the Earth,

A CEIBA TREE impressively rooted in the tropical jungle, which covered most of the non-coastal areas where the Maya lived during the Classic era. The Maya call the tree *yaxche* ("first tree"). The ceiba bears fruit around the March equinox, just before maize is planted, connecting the myth of creation to the life cycle of the ceiba and the movements of the Milky Way.

the four sides, the four corners,
as it is said,
by the Maker, Modeller,
mother-father of life, of humankind
giver of breath, giver of heart . . ."

Literally a people of maize, the Maya clearly saw the world around them, in an intimate and harmonious way, as a four-sided maize field. They believed that this ideal world was so because the universe was held in sublime balance by means of natural and supernatural aspects. Because things are a combination of movement and number, everything was held in a state of order and its life and movements were as predictable as the sun, moon, stars and planets. The "heavens" were, therefore, the obvious pattern for human life on Earth, which must be held together by the same balance and harmony as the solar system, and by the same energy.

However, this balance and harmony was not always evident: the Mayan peoples were frequently in conflict and in the heavens the cycles of the Earth, sun and moon could not be synchronized in such a way that they could be neatly represented by one of the Mayan calendars. Perhaps the Maya's consciousness of such imperfections lay behind their concept of change and evolution: the hope that every recurring cycle would advance them to better things. Of equal importance was the Maya's acute sense of place in the greater scheme, their connection to which was symbolized by the Milky Way, visible above them, and the ceiba tree, a constant presence in their everyday lives and the central axis of the world around them.

THE SKY AT SUNSET

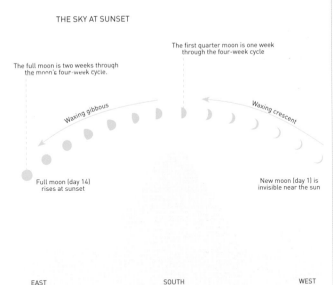

The first quarter moon is one week through the four-week cycle

The full moon is two weeks through the moon's four-week cycle.

Waxing gibbous

Waxing crescent

Full moon (day 14) rises at sunset

New moon (day 1) is invisible near the sun

EAST   SOUTH   WEST

The Maya share with many other cultures a rich and obsessive mythological attachment to the moon, but the Maya's interest was such that they gave the moon its own calendar, known as the Tun-Uc. The prophecy related to the cycles of the moon's phases in the *katun* ending in 2012 is one whose message is less than positive. The moon's character of deceitfulness, promiscuity and unpredictability suggests events that will both surprise and challenge us. The moon's association with water implies periods of disastrously destructive flooding. Where Westerners are familiar with the image of the "man in the moon", the Maya identify the satellite with a moon goddess and see a "rabbit in the moon", which is linked with drunkenness and thus a humanity intoxicated with pleasure and materialism, but also in search of deeper satisfaction and contentment. In sharp contrast, the moon's connection to childbirth suggests a more positive future, perhaps through the emergence of a new, sensitive

8.
PROPHECIES RELATED TO THE MOON

When the invasion came during Katun 11 Ahau, even the heavens pitied themselves. They blamed it on the moon when our warriors cut their own throats.

This is the flower of the night . . . a star in the sky. This is the vile thing of the night: it is the moon.

Book of Chilam Balam of Chumayel

Then when 5 Ahau arrived on his [the year-bearer's] day within the year 5 Muluc, there was a crescent moon, omen of life.

Book of Chilam Balam of Tizimin

and more cosmically conscious humanity. A practical edge is given to this prophecy through lunar associations with both weaving (see page 100) and agriculture. The extremes are clear, the outcome is in the balance.

THE LUNAR CALENDAR

The Tun-Uc (*tun* is "count" and *uc* is "moon") is a calendar that is based on twelve lunar (synodical) months. A lunar month was calculated from new moon to new moon, giving an average of 29.5 days and therefore 354 days for the lunar year. However, to coordinate the Tun-Uc with the moon's phases the Maya alternated the length of the months between twenty-nine and thirty days, but this still gave the same total number of 354, which is, of course, shorter than the actual solar year (365¼ days). As a result, the lunar year was not linked to the changing seasons because the Maya did not use intercalary months, as the

THE PORTENTS OF ECLIPSES

 There will be two eclipses of the sun during 2012. The first will be on 20 March when the sun and the moon will conjunct with the Pleiades (the rattle in the snake's tail); the second on 13 November, when the sun and moon will conjunct with the constellation Serpens (the Serpent).

Eclipse tables are of great importance to Mayan astronomers. The most complete examples, in the *Dresden Codex*, cover a cycle of 405 lunations of 29.53 day-lengths – that is 11,960 days. By the mid-eighth century CE, and possibly much earlier, the Maya had discovered that eclipses, lunar and solar, could only occur within plus or minus eighteen days of the node (when the moon's path crosses the apparent path of the sun). Because the Maya were aware of precession, it is likely that their tables were remade every fifty years or so.

The eclipse glyph recurs frequently in the codices and it was believed that eclipses influenced historical events, being divine signs of good or bad fortune. Interestingly, the *Dresden Codex* symbol of the eclipse is a snake biting the sun. The Mayan word for "eclipse", *chibil*, means "eaten" – thus, the moon eats the sun, or the Earth eats both of them. Another myth has ants eating the sun or moon during an eclipse.

The belief survives today that an eclipse is a battle between the sun and the moon. In folklore, a pregnant woman may deform her foetus if she looks at an eclipse. There is a belief among the Lacandon Maya that the destructions of the world in previous eras all began with an eclipse, and a total eclipse will precede the end of the world.

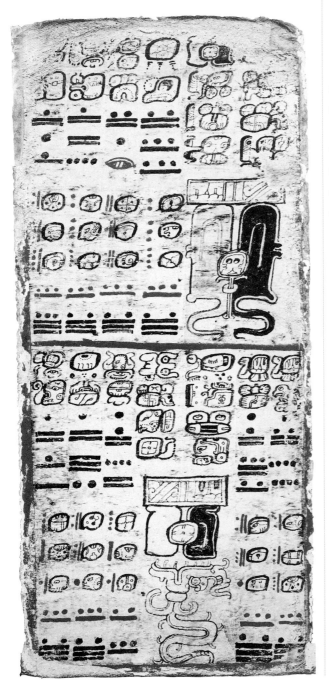

Gregorian calendar does, to synchronize the lunar cycles with the solar year.

The Maya seem to have gone to a great deal of trouble to rationalize the lunar calendar, and the Tun-Uc was supplemented by what are known as "the lunar glyphs". A series of eight of these have been found on stelae, added as inscriptions to the Long Count calendar – and they are in fact the oldest of the Maya's astronomical records. The glyphs record a specific date on the Tun-Uc, the name of the current lunar month, its length and the number of days elapsed since the last new moon. The glyphs reveal that the Maya sought to keep track of the age of the moon – in days – during each month, as well as of the moon's changing phases. In addition, they were able to calculate the times of the conjunctions of the moon with Venus.

These lunar phases were integrated with the 260-day *tzolkin* calendar, with the result that the moon imposed itself on the "character" of the day, resulting in times that were deemed the most suitable, or propitious, for certain activities, such as medicine, childbirth and weaving. Images and texts survive which describe the "burden" of the moon goddess on a particular day. Thus, the moon influenced the daily lives of the Mayan people, with the Tun-Uc being used to designate the best days for religious ceremonies and for predictions by the shaman-priests.

THE *DRESDEN CODEX* contains highly accurate astronomical tables and has chapters on the moon goddess and her influence. It is best known for its Venus table and its lunar series, which includes tables that predict when solar and lunar eclipses will occur – this page (left) shows two eclipses as white-and-black shapes (top page, bottom right and bottom page, centre) around a moon or sun symbol.

José Argüelles has suggested that we should adopt the lunar calendar of thirteen months, each with twenty-eight days, to give a year of 364 days. A calendar based on this would conform to the natural cycles of the moon and the sun – that is, every time the Earth goes around the sun, the moon goes around the Earth thirteen times. We have noted that the numbers thirteen and twenty carry a range of symbolic references for the Maya, and they combine to make up the 260-day Sacred Count of the *tzolkin* and the Long Count calendars.

It is easy to see why the thirteen-month lunar calendar is a natural alternative to the Gregorian calendar. It would not oblige us to change radically our perception of time from a linear pattern to a cyclic pattern, but this shift to the lunar cycle (which already influences our lives through the tides) would be a creative start.

Such a calendar would take us from artificial to natural time, from an anarchy of time to the unity of time, from a world splintered by the conflicts of competing civil and religious calendars to a world that shares the same calendar as a paradigm for greater unity and peace. In short, our map of time would change significantly, and – by habit – so eventually would our consciousness. Of greater importance is the awareness that if time exists in the mind, then a dysfunctional map of time will have a debilitating effect on the mind. Is it possible that the arbitrary calendar, which programmes everything we do, is setting up all kinds of tensions by steering us away from a natural and harmonious alternative?

THE MOON GODDESS

Various divinities are associated with the moon, but none more so than the young goddess depicted in a glyph sitting on the crescent moon, holding a rabbit in her arms. This is a reference to a myth in which the first moon was as bright as the sun, and in an attempt to dull its glare the deities hurled a rabbit into its face. The unnamed young woman is sometimes mistakenly called Ixchel, who is another, more elderly mother goddess, and wife of Itzamná. Some of the confusion may arise from the association of different goddesses with phases of the moon – a youthful figure for the waxing moon and a mature one for the waning moon.

The myth of the attractive, youthful goddess prevails, and the moon retains its associations with menstruation and fertility. The older moon goddess, Ixchel, is also the patron of weaving – she is believed to have invented the technique of backstrap weaving and is sometimes depicted with one end of her loom tied to a tree and the other bound around her waist. This craft is still practised widely in the Guatemalan Highlands, where many high-quality textiles are produced. Before work begins, sacrifices are made to the goddess. Weaving is a symbol of the vital connectedness of the Mayan woman, who is at one with her environment. The image perfectly illustrates one of the running themes of the prophecies: to solve the problems of our planet, we need to recover a closer integration with nature.

THE MOON GODDESS astride a deer is a regional variation of the same goddess with a rabbit. A Mayan myth explains that by stepping on the goddess's abdomen the deer created a vagina, enabling her to bear the children of the sun god.

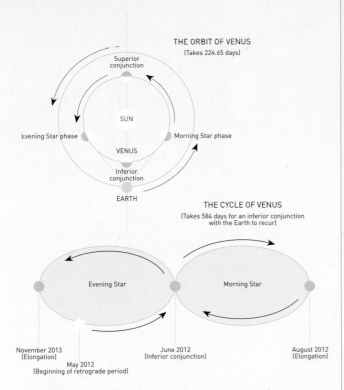

THE ORBIT OF VENUS
(Takes 224.65 days)

Superior
conjunction

SUN

Evening Star phase

Morning Star phase

VENUS

Inferior
conjunction

EARTH

THE CYCLE OF VENUS
(Takes 584 days for an inferior conjunction
with the Earth to recur)

Evening Star

Morning Star

November 2013
(Elongation)

May 2012
(Beginning of retrograde period)

June 2012
(Inferior conjunction)

August 2012
(Elongation)

9.
PROPHECY RELATED TO VENUS

Venus is fixed in the Western mind as the Roman goddess of love. After the moon, Venus is the second strongest light in the night sky, at its brightest just before sunrise and just after sunset – for which reason it is sometimes known as the "morning and evening star". The planet established its feminine reputation early on, figuring thousands of years ago in Babylonian texts as the personification of womanhood. The morning and evening showings of Venus were read by Egyptian astronomers as different stars, but the Hellenic Greeks and the Maya knew that these were of one and the same star. Although Venus's femininity may be central to Western astrology, to the Maya the planet was a masculine, baleful symbol under the influence of a violent, spear-carrying deity (Lahun Chan, often depicted with the head of a jaguar and the body of a dog) and its presence can herald the onset of malign forces such as famines, droughts, wars, and so on. Venus was also said to be a manifestation of Kukulcan.

> *There they looked for the coming forth of the sun . . . then they fasted and cried out in prayer. They fixed their eyes firmly on their dawn, looking there to the east. They watched closely for the Morning Star, the Great Star that gives its light at the birth of the sun. They looked to the womb of the sky and the womb of the Earth.*

Popul Vuh

> *The sight of Venus on the sun is by far the noblest that astronomy can afford.*

Edmund Halley, Astronomer Royal, 1691

(PREVIOUS PAGES) The Nunnery Quadrangle at Uxmal was a governor's palace (the modern name derives from the Spanish nickname). This facade is decorated with double-headed serpent bars, which would once have been painted. The corner carvings are of masks and glyphs, which include the symbol for Venus.

With the role and reputation of the planet reversed when compared with Western astrology, Venus was the Mayan equivalent of Mars and its prophecy is clearly one of various forms of impending conflict and disaster. Such dangerous portents meant that Venus and its cycles were of great importance and played a central role in Mayan astronomy. The start date of the Long Count itself on 13 August 3114BCE was sometimes referred to as the "birth of Venus", though the end-date does not signify its demise.

Mayan astronomers had several main centres from which to monitor Venus. At Chichén Itzá, the circular Caracol (see page 67) was built as an observatory specifically to record the movements of Venus. At Uxmal, the Nunnery Quadrangle complex has 584 windows to match the number of days in a Venus cycle, and the Palace of the Governors, the site's finest architectural structure, has more than 350 Venus-related glyphs adorning it.

THE MALIGN WASP STAR

The Maya called Venus Noh Ek ("the Great Star") or Xux Ek ("the Wasp Star"). The vital statistics of its astronomy are recorded in the *Dresden Codex*, and despite Mayan misgivings the rhythm of the planet's movements suggest harmony. As John Martineau has written, as the planet passes between Earth and the sun, "Venus rotates extremely slowly on her own axis in the opposite direction to most rotations in the solar system. Her day is precisely two-thirds of an Earth year, a musical fifth. . . . every time Venus and the Earth kiss, Venus does so with the same face."

At its minimum distance of 67.2 million miles (108 million km) Venus is the second closest planet to the sun. (Mercury is the nearest at 36 million miles/58 million km.) Venus's journey round the sun is an almost circular orbit which takes about 225 Earth days, compared to the Earth's orbit of 365 days. It takes a cycle of 584 days for Venus – in a figure-of-eight cycle – to pass between us and the sun and it is this passage of the planet across the face of the sun that is called a transit of Venus (see diagram, page 103).

Eight Earth years equals thirteen Venus years, and every 243 of our years Venus passes between the Earth and the sun twice in eight years. For example, two paired transits occurred during in 1761 and 1769. The first of a pair of transits took place 243 years later, on 8 June 2004, and the second will occur 243 years after the 1769 transit, on 6 June 2012. It is interesting to note that these 243-year cycles parallel exactly the number of days it takes the slow-turning Venus to rotate around its own axis, and that during those 243 years exactly 365 Venus days will have passed. This can be written off as a solar coincidence or else a different possibility can be considered – that, as Carl Calleman argues: ". . . this is a type of primal synchronicity which is linked to the fact that Venus has been created as the mirror of the Earth, and maybe in the year 2012, as our consciousness has become more cosmic, this will simply be seen by us as self-explanatory."

VENUS TERROR

The malign influence of Venus was most potent at the heliacal rising (when the planet first becomes visible above the eastern horizon just before sunrise) and setting. But why should it be that certain astronomical conditions were believed to be so dangerous that human life had to be offered to avert calamity? Professor Ronald Bonewitz believes that the solution lies in a precedent: ". . . some dreadful celestial event in the past, at a time when Venus was prominent to the Maya . . . an event that affected many civilizations worldwide . . . Few celestial happenings could strike such terror into the hearts of men, but an impact of a comet or its fragments is certainly one of them."

If this thesis is correct, Venus was associated with a catastrophic event in early Mayan history – perhaps a comet impact, massive flooding or an earthquake that occurred at the time of a Venus transit. Prophecies of similar events would then have been read into future reappearances of Venus. Accurately recorded in the almanacs, these would have been tied in to the repetition of the twenty-year *katun* during which the original event took place. In this way the drastic Venus-related tradition

A JAINA ISLAND MAYAN WARRIOR in a feather costume. His fierce look hints at a formidable foe, whose campaigns in battle would have been influenced by the movements of Venus. Clay figure, c.800CE, painted blue as a funerary offering.

of human sacrifice might have been established as the only way to prevent a catastrophic recurrence. It is clear that Venus was perceived by the Maya to exude malevolence. Curiously, we now know that it has an otherness because it revolves in the opposite direction to the other major planets. The threat that the planet appears to pose is balanced by its associations with the return of Kukulcan at a time when humankind will be in the greatest need.

Whatever it was that determined the Mayan view of Venus, the fear ran deep in their mythic consciousness. It seems that when the planet rose, they closed their doors and windows against its malevolent light, believing it to be the carrier of ill-fortune and sickness. The worst days, when all of nature was under threat, were when Venus rose after an inferior conjunction. The image used is of Venus as a hurled spear, and a codex lists the spear's targets on specific days, such as the aged, the lords, the young, and rain (or lack of it, causing drought).

As already mentioned, the planet was identified with Kukulcan. The "feathered" or "plumed" serpent was associated with war, and in Mayan mythology Kukulcan had sacrificed himself by plunging into fire, as Venus seems to do when it transits the sun. Belief in the return of Kukulcan, figured in the cycles of Venus, was central to the cult that had spread throughout Mesoamerica. Venus has other personifications, one of them being that of a

KING CHAN-MUAN OF BONAMPAK, wearing a jaguar pelt as a symbol of his authority, seizes an adversary by the hair (whose broken spear signifies his defeat) during a raid for sacrificial victims. Computer-enhanced rendering of the ancient mural in Bonampak's Room 2.

"shining warrior from the east", clearly a reference to the morning star. The *Grolier Codex* has an image of a skeletal Venus on the point of beheading a prisoner, thought to be an efficacious sacrifice before waging war. The creation myth in the *Popul Vuh* calls Venus "Icoquih", meaning "she who carries the sun on her shoulders".

Reinforcing the Mayan Mars analogy, the position of Venus was used to find an auspicious date for the launch of a military campaign and inscriptions record that an evening rising of Venus was used as the signal for an attack. The sight of Venus signalling the start of a battle was also the moment to sacrifice prisoners taken from any previous wars. In fact, it is thought that some wars were waged purely for the purpose of stocking up on captives for future use in sacrifices to Venus. The higher the rank of a captive, the more efficacious the offering. One prisoner, a ruler called Siebal, was kept alive for twelve years in order to be sacrificed at a certain conjunction with Venus.

The "shining warrior" epithet relates to Classic Mayan inscriptions referring to "star wars" – that is, wars triggered by Venus's movements, sometimes in conjunction with Jupiter. The Maya also recorded the planet's maximum brightness and elongation, both as the morning and the evening star. The best time for battle was when Venus rose for the first time after its inferior or superior conjunction, and it seems that wars thus timed were the most violent and brutal of all. Such conflicts became more frequent in the eighth century and their destructiveness may have contributed to the downfall of Mayan civilization.

10.
TRANSITION TO A NEW AGE

Then the creation dawned upon the world. During the creation thirteen infinite series [steps] added to seven was the count of the creation of the world. Then a new world dawned for them.

Book of Chilam Balam of Chumayel

The Mayan fifth world age is drawing to a close. The sixth will begin in 2012, marking the start of a new great cycle of time and the resetting of the clock of precession. We are, thus, between ages – in a period known as the "apocalypse": a time of revelation or disclosure. This prophecy combines with others that speak of the recovery of ancient wisdom, the assimilation of new truths and the opportunity that humanity will have to work out its problems responsibly by the choices it makes.

This theme of the transition of our civilization into a new age is the most familiar one running through the prophecies, contradicting the sensationalist "end-of-the-world" scenario. The energy of the prophecy is taken from the modern form of Mayan astrology, which describes "age" transitions as stages in humanity's development.

The Mayan astrological age, determined by the precession of the equinoxes, is, as we have seen, a cycle of approximately 26,000 years. This figure of 26,000 years

HUNAHPÚ AND XBALANQUÉ, the ancestral hero twins, as they were named in the *Popol Vuh*, depicted on a vase alongside an assortment of animals, including several from the Mayan zodiac, such as the dog, rabbit, bat and owl. The actions of the twins in outwitting the lords of death ensured that it was the human form of godhood that ultimately spanned the worlds of existence.

(which is more precisely 25,630 solar years) is divided by the Maya into five periods called the Five Suns, each with 5,200 *tun* years (thirteen *baktun*s of about 400 *tun* years/394 solar years each), equivalent to 5,126 solar years.

THE AGE OF FIVE SUNS

Each of these four past world ages, or creative cycles, is believed to have ended in some form of (unspecified) disaster. The dates for these four ages are as follows:

First Sun: 23,618–18,492BCE
Second Sun: 18,492–13,366BCE
Third Sun: 13,366–8240BCE
Fourth Sun: 8240–3114BCE

We live in the age of the Fifth Sun, which began in 3114BCE and will draw to a close in 2012CE.

The mythology of the Maya recounted in the *Popul Vuh* (*Book of the Community*) explains how the first humans were created during the age of the First Sun. Modern geological records show that the Earth was still affected by a glacial age that endangered the lives of large mammals. There is no evidence that the period ended with a global disaster that annihilated life, but a more localized disaster would have been enough to have had an impact on the ancestors of the Maya and influenced their oral tradition.

Whatever natural disasters occurred, they did not happen precisely on the end-date of each world age. Instead, there may have been an extreme process underway toward the end of one age which overlapped with and continued into the next. The period at the close of the First Sun and the beginning of the Second Sun may have been one with extreme climate changes that led to the retreat of the ice and the need for human beings to adapt to new environments. The close of the second cycle may have seen the end of the ice age and flooding.

During the third cycle humans began to settle and early forms of agriculture began to displace hunter gathering. What disasters there were, such as more flooding and volcanic activity, will have been regional rather than global. The age of the Fourth Sun may have followed a similar pattern during which fertile land gave way to deserts, and huge floods occurred of the kind recorded in the book of Genesis, but again these are likely to have been relatively local events.

The opening of the age of the Fifth Sun marked the start date of the Long Count calendar that will end in 2012. The prophecies for the end-date clearly point to a new world age, a turning toward a Sixth Sun when we can say, "A new day will dawn". But we also turn toward the first *katun* of the first sun of another cycle of five suns, and the 26,000 years of a new precessional sequence.

In Mayan cosmology 21 December 2012 is the end of the Fifth Sun, which raises the question, are we to expect some form of disaster? Mythology is often the abstraction of real events, accounts of which form an oral tradition

that was laid down in a period greatly distanced from the culture destined to be the tradition's custodian. Mythology is like the echo of a memory, an atavistic intuition that holds us to a continuum of meaning and helps to make mystery comprehensible. The Mayan prophecy of the current world age ending in disaster is founded on such mythologies, but we can suppose that behind them were actual events. The world will not end, but our transition to the new age may be uncomfortable.

MAYAN ASTROLOGY

The best astrology is a science, and although the Mayan astrologers realized this, in their system science and mysticism are so interrelated that it is not always possible for us to read the astrology clearly. The *Dresden Codex* is mostly taken up with astrological charts and almanacs, calculations and predictions, based mainly on the 584-day Venus cycle. However, the roots of Mayan astrology and the Mayan zodiac are based on the influence of the sun, which is why the Mayan astrologer-priests were also known as sun-priests.

The zodiac is like the face of a clock: it offers a method of reading the "signs" and the "times" together. It is not a coincidence that the Maya predicted that during the *katun* leading to 2012

A HUNTER WITH A DEER that will provide meat and hides, depicted on a Mayan ceramic bowl. Because deer were most active after dusk the Maya associated them with the moon goddess. In Mayan cosmology, both the deer and the peccary were linked with agriculture, fertility, seasonal renewal and annual transition.

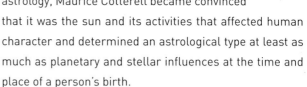

there would be unprecedented sunspot activity, and an increase in solar winds (see pages 149–153), both of which will affect the Earth and its magnetic poles. Having researched Mayan astrology, Maurice Cotterell became convinced that it was the sun and its activities that affected human character and determined an astrological type at least as much as planetary and stellar influences at the time and place of a person's birth.

A Mayan "horoscope" reading covers complementary signs, harmonious signs and offers a life analysis based on the characteristics associated with these signs. The zodiacal signs (see page 116) were related to the day-names of the *tzolkin* (the sacred cycle or count of days), each day-sign carrying a range of significances and associations. The influences of the day-signs will vary positively and negatively according to how the day-number (for example, 1 Imix) of the *tzolkin* interrelates with the *haab* (see pages 22–27). As an example of how this works, let us consider Imix, the first day of the twenty:

The Glyph Imix: Represents a container of water, also rain and the spirit of rain.

Associations: World, water lily, alligator and the reptilian body of the planet Earth or the world.

Significance: It makes the mind reflective, increases spiritual strength, enables the person to cope with change and to understand nature. It represents everything that corresponds to the subtle aspects of human nature. The agricultural calendar begins with this day.

THE 20 DAY NAMES AND GLYPHS OF A *TUN* MONTH WITH THEIR ASSOCIATIONS

 **IMIX** (1 of 20) World, water lily, alligator, the reptilian body of planet Earth.

 IK (2) Air, wind, breath and life; also, violence.

 AKBAL (3) "Night-house", or darkness, the Underworld; also, evil.

 KAN (4) Maize, seed, Maize Lord who brings abundance, ripeness; also, lizard, net.

 CHIKCHAN (5) Snake, the celestial serpent.

 KIMI (6) Death.

 MANIK (7) Deer, sign of the Lord of the Hunt; also, hand.

 LAMAT (8) Rabbit, sign of the planet Venus; also, sunset.

 MULUC (9) Water, symbolized by jade; also, rain and fish.

 OK (10) Dog, the sun's guide through the Underworld.

 CHUWEN (11) Monkey, great craftsman, patron of arts and knowledge; also, thread.

 EB (12) Grass, or point, associated with rain, storms; also, tooth, road.

 BEN (13) Reed – who fosters the growth of corn, cane and man.

 IX (14) Jaguar – the night sun; also, maize.

 MEN (15) Eagle, the wise one, bird, moon.

 KIB (16) Vulture, owl – death-birds of night and day; also, soul, wax, insect.

 KABAN (17) Earthquake, thus formidable power. Also, season, earth, thought.

 ETZNAB (18) Knife, flint, the obsidian sacrificial blade.

 KAWAC (19) Storm or rain – celestial dragon, serpents, gods of thunder and lightning.

 AHAU (20) Lord, the radiant sun god; also, light.

Characteristics: People born on this day are home-loving, spiritual, sociable and adaptable, warm, caring and romantic. They may also be daring and eccentric, with strong personalities that are sensitive to mystical vibrations.

Positive aspects: Truthful, energetic, creative and productive. Sensitive to "cosmic messages".

Negative aspects: Tend to be indecisive and disorganized. Temperamental and susceptible to mental disorders.

Energy: Imix is a day that brings the right kind of energy for increasing spiritual power. It is the best day on which to ask for rain and the purification of water.

Professions: Teachers, psychologists, sociologists, doctors, artists, poets, judges, spiritual healers and priests.

Body parts: Imix people tend to be governed by their blood, ganglia and genitalia.

Animal associations: Lizard, crocodile, shark, turtle.

Colours: Yellow, green, light blue.

The *tzolkin* is still used in the calendars kept by Mayan day-keepers throughout the Yucatán, Guatemala, Belize and Honduras, and in the practice of divination. The *tzolkin* may be thought of as a twenty-day week cycled thirteen times, which then repeats.

Today it is possible for anyone, anywhere in the world, to consult a specialist website and ascertain their Mayan sign, then acquire a Mayan horoscope reading. Famous people born under Imix include Claude Monet, Thomas Edison, Walt Disney, Frank Sinatra, Federico Fellini, King Juan Carlos I and Tom Hanks.

THE ANIMAL ZODIAC

The Maya have an interesting animal zodiac, but the scorpion is the only creature it has in common with the Western zodiac, though it has three in common with the Chinese system (monkey, dog and rabbit). The Mayan animals are associated with the "thirteen-moon natural time" calendar, still used by Mayan communities in the Guatemalan highlands, and are as follows: bat, scorpion, deer, owl, peacock, lizard, monkey, hawk, jaguar, dog, rabbit and turtle.

Each animal had an important role in Mayan mythology and certain associated characteristics. The bat represents unity and purpose; the scorpion is polarizing, stabilizing and challenging; the deer is active, bonding and offering service; the owl is analytical, influencing form and measurement; the peacock is radiance, power and leadership; the lizard is organization, balance and equality; the monkey is channelling, inspiring and harmonious; the hawk is unifying, a role-model and integrity; the jaguar is the pulse or beat of life, realization and intention; the dog is perfectionist, productive, exemplary; the serpent is terminating and liberating; the rabbit is dedication, cooperation and inspiring unity; the turtle is endurance, transcendence and presence.

Our need of a closer relationship with nature is a theme that runs through the prophecies. Observing the patterns of behaviour in the natural world and absorbing them into our lives will help us to recover that long-lost connection. In this way we may be better placed to make the transition into a new age.

11.
UNITY OF HUMANKIND

> *Sufficient in themselves are my words, for I am* chilam balam, *the jaguar priest. I repeat my words of divine truth: I say that the divisions of the Earth shall be one! This is the ninth year of Katun 1 Ahau.*

Book of Chilam Balam of Tizimin

This prophecy indicates that as we move toward 2012, it will become increasingly apparent that the various races, religions and classes that divide us mask an essential unity, and that despite conflicts, people will be drawn closer together. The prophecy makes it clear that only by realizing its inherent togetherness can humanity solve the problems facing our planet and its civilization. It has been said that as the things of the world break up, the things of the spirit gather together, and the Mayan elders regard this prophecy about the unity of humankind as already in the process of being fulfilled. The last century saw the end of segregation in the United States and of apartheid in South Africa, many historically class-bound societies have become more egalitarian, in religion there are influential ecumenical movements, and all the major religions have responded to the work of the Council for a Parliament of the World's Religions. The prophecy of unity, however, is cast in broader terms.

The ancient Maya were far from being a role model of a united people. They had no central, unifying authority and their nation consisted of loosely associated city-states. Approximately twenty independent states spread across what is now Guatemala, the Yucatán and southern Mexico were held precariously together by nothing more substantial than a common culture.

Mayan society was rigidly hierarchical, founded on a hereditary class structure which bound the populace to the status into which they had been born. At the base of the social pyramid was a humble labouring and farming class; above that, a form of middle class, consisting of scribes, priests and architects; and beyond them an educated class of administrators and provincial governors who served a hereditary absolute monarchy. The hierarchy was literally written in stone – the genealogy of the kings being copiously recorded on the buildings and stelae of all the major temple complexes. Even as their civilization flourished, the city-states were frequently at war with each other, fighting over boundaries, or simply to take captives for sacrifice. Any periods of peace were almost certainly only brief. There were times when common problems, such as crop failures, natural catastrophes and forest fires or outbreaks of disease, would have distracted the city-states from their conflicts, and perhaps drawn them together to face the common challenge.

DISEASE – THE ENEMY OF ALL

 Disease is one of several shared threats that would, at times, have blunted the sharp differences between the Mayan city-states. There are references in the codices to "blood vomit", and many diseases were the product of climate change, brought about by deforestation and the altered pattern of rainfall.

Diseases were believed to be caused by gods living in the Underworld or inflicted by sorcery. Devastating smallpox plagues raged through Mayan societies in the wake of the Spanish conquest, which left the Maya in no doubt that the worst diseases were inflicted on them by the Spaniards. "There was then no sickness . . . at that time the course of humanity was orderly. The foreigners made it otherwise when they arrived here."

More importantly, any disease was thought to signify an imbalance between the inflicted people, and the natural and spirit world around them. The prophecy of the unity of mankind seems born of the Maya's own experiences. It speaks to us as a warning – that faced with a common threat, the only hope is to set aside our own inveterate conflicts and face the threat together.

VISION OF SHARED HUMANITY

The kind of unity that will help us to solve today's problems goes beyond class, sectarian and religious divisions. It points to an outward-looking interfaith dialogue and to mutuality based on our shared humanity.

The prophecy is partly confirmed by events such as the 1995 pilgrimage to Chichén Itzá, led by Hunbatz Men, attended by Tibetan *lamas* and the Wisdom Conservancy, which promotes the cultures and sacred knowledge of indigenous people. One of the incentives that will encourage people to overcome their conditioned differences is the retrieval of ancient knowledge and wisdom buried beneath centuries of materialism.

The surest path to overcoming our differences is for humanity to re-establish its proper relationship with nature. In 1994 the then president of the Czech Republic Václav Havel summed up the task as follows: "Planetary democracy does not yet exist, but our global civilization is already preparing a place for it: it is the very Earth we inhabit, linked with Heaven above us. Only in this setting can the mutuality and the commonalty of the human race be newly created, with reverence and gratitude for that which transcends each of us, and all of us together. The authority of a world democratic order simply cannot be built on anything else but the revitalized authority of the universe."

A MEMBER OF THE MAYAN ELITE is depicted in his distinctive bulky costume, elaborate headdress and complex backrack. This attire provided symbolic meaning as well as visual drama, with various deities depicted to emphasize the wearer's status as someone with a divine right to rule. Jaina pottery figure.

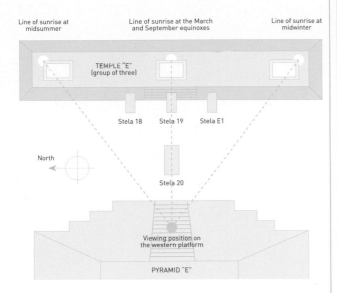

PLAZA OF SOLAR ALIGNMENTS
AT GROUP "E", UAXACTÚN

Line of sunrise at midsummer

Line of sunrise at the March and September equinoxes

Line of sunrise at midwinter

TEMPLE "E"
(group of three)

Stela 18 Stela 19 Stela E1

North

Stela 20

Viewing position on
the western platform

PYRAMID "E"

12.
A NEW ENLIGHTENMENT

Your souls shall accept the truth and hold it in high esteem . . . It will come to pass that you shall adore the divine truth, and the government of our ancestors will stand in readiness forever.

The Prophecy of Yabun Chuan

This prophecy points to a time when there will be a radical change in human values and perceptions. Our understanding of who we are will deepen, requiring us to reconsider the purpose of life, our relationship with nature, and with each other. The prophecy anticipates that people will "accept the truth", value it and adjust their lives accordingly. "Enlightenment" is seeing and accepting the truth about the nature of life, the planet on which we live and the universe as a whole. This is not a matter for the intellect alone: it is something that must touch our lives at the most basic levels of our priorities and moral values. Rather than a sudden revelation, "enlightenment" is more often a gradual but deep realization of the truth of things. The prophet Yabun Chuan goes on to affirm that humanity "will begin to esteem our learning and our knowledge of the unrolling of the face of the universe. . . ."

It is difficult for the Western rationalist mind to understand the place of enlightenment in Mayan culture

– a society that was brutal and cruel, with human sacrifice practised. The best we can do is to understand that the Maya were a society in transition. Their sense of the world was more holistic than ours: from their naked-eye observation of the skies to their relationship with maize, everything held together. Animism made nature a gallery of gods; the Maya were as much in touch with the spirit world as we are with the material world.

Enlightenment implies the acquisition of knowledge – ranging from a concern with abstract concepts to a nuts-and-bolts search for everyday wisdom. Every aspect of Mayan life was concerned with "knowing"; their culture of

THE SUN GOD KINICH AHAU on a funerary urn, with a feline head – probably a jaguar's – as its lid. The god has barbels, a reference to the part-catfish creatures the Hero Twins became after being sacrificed. Painted clay (detail), c.600–900CE.

prophecy was about accessing certain kinds of knowledge in a particular way. The seeking of knowledge was woven into day-to-day existence. Shaman-diviners were consulted over marriage, business, agriculture, politics and so on. The omnipresence of the gods – manifest as trees, animals, wind, rain, the sun, moon, stars, planets, and even diseases – constantly reminded the Maya that divinely sourced knowledge was always potentially available.

This prophecy, however, is mainly concerned with enlightenment in the form of what Buddhists might call an "awakening". Contemporary Mayan elders, while acknowledging the possibility of "immediate perception", tell us that for most people the truth will come through teaching and reflection – a progressive revelation that will contribute to our individual and collective maturity.

THE SUN AND ENLIGHTENMENT

The Mayan sun god was known as Kinich Ahau, meaning "sun-faced" or "sun-eyed" lord. He was lord of the day, while the moon was lord of the night. The sun god's iconography is closely linked to the calendar: his eyeballs are glyphs for the *winal*, the twenty-day month, his headdress has an image of the *katun*.

Another motif is the two-headed serpent, symbolic of the heavenly vault. Ahau is the last day of the Mayan ritual calendar and it was dedicated to Kinich Ahau as a manifestation of Itzamná, the supreme deity.

As the "star of life", the sun god was the source of all knowledge, both relative and absolute. The sun's daily "enlightenment" journey, from sunrise to sunset, corresponds to the human passage through life. The Maya lived in fear that the sun would cease to rise, an obsession that was acted out dramatically in the ballcourt (see page 35).

13.
COSMIC CONSCIOUSNESS

> *Only through solar initiation can the sleeping body of mankind be awakened . . . Let us prepare to receive the light of knowledge that comes from Hunab Ku, and transcend into the memory of the Creator and become beings of eternal luminosity.*

The Sacred Manuscript of K'altun

Initiation into what might be interpreted as a special kind of arcane, mysterious wisdom is not something that most people would seek out. The solar initiation event held in 1995 at Chichén Itzá, and led by Hunbatz Men, is an example of a contemporary Mayan initiation, but it was one that was open to all – there was never any sense that it was a hidden, secretive rite to which only a privileged few had access. No Mayan elder would wish to represent a teaching that is out of reach to ordinary people, even if his audience were children.

Although "the light of knowledge" can be thought of as a mental transformation – perhaps one imagined to have been wrought in an instant by Chac's lightning-axe – references to transcendence can be problematic for many Westerners because this language carries overtones of the LSD-fuelled 1960s counterculture and its search for "cosmic consciousness". But this prophecy bears no resemblance to a transient hippie trip. The prophecy speaks of a certain quality of awareness, a sense of the wholeness of the extended environment in which we live – one that will give us the feeling of being "at home" in the visible universe in much the same way that we are in our own living rooms.

Being cosmically conscious is, in fact, a consequence of the previous prophecy, which predicts the true enlightenment of increasing numbers of people.

THE COSMOS REAL AND IMAGINED

To the Maya the cosmos was the whole observable universe, from the immediate earthly environment in which people lived their lives to "the Great Mother in the sky – the cosmic birther and source of manifestation . . . the bright, wide part of the Milky Way near Sagittarius . . . the womb of the sky." It was critical for the Maya that they should be aware of the galactic centre, located in the Milky

THE CROCODILIAN COSMIC MONSTER

The Cosmic Monster was often depicted as a huge dragon-like reptile, similar to a crocodile. It represents the great arch in the sky formed by the curve of the Milky Way when it runs from east to west. On many carved panels and stelae, a king holds a Vision Serpent, the body of which merges with a skyband depicting the Cosmic Monster, its head marked with Venus signs. The monster is especially associated with the sun and Venus as they move through space. That the Milky Way is suggestive of both the Cosmic Mother and the Cosmic Monster is an odd juxtaposition. It has been

suggested that any variation in depictions of the monster's body form may arise because they represent different parts of the Milky Way – an Underworld and Upper World dichotomy. The body parts may show different constellations, while the skyband (a narrow band used in Mayan art to symbolize the cosmic realm) illustrates the location at which the ecliptic of the sun crosses the Milky Way – that point, in the southern sky, when the sun is "reborn" at dawn on the winter solstice, following the longest night of the year. These different mythic identities are not

meant to be reconciled: each is an opposing energy – one of all things creative, and one of all things threatening. The monster, its mouth the entrance to the Underworld, through its association with Venus carries the threat of some huge natural disaster, and the fear that the sun may not rise again.

At Palenque stucco reliefs from House E depict a cosmic monster with a *kin* (sun) in the middle of its body and an upside-down quadripartite badge at its tail end; another shows a two-headed saurian or reptile.

A WATER LILY MONSTER in the form of a skeletal god, with a turtle carapace for its body, holds a large bone over its head while it is surrounded by water lilies and fish-eating flowers. Associated with the underworld realm, the water lily symbolized life after death and movements between the cosmic worlds. The plant was also a source of hallucinogens for the ancient Maya, which means it appears frequently in Mayan iconography. Painted vase.

Way. "Cosmos" is, therefore, both a reality and a mythological theme central to Mayan culture, which was heavily represented in Mayan iconography (see box, opposite). The cosmos was envisaged as both a monster and a tree, the monster being snake-like and the tree being the World Tree, *wacah chan*, whose trunk splits to become the Vision Serpent (see page 75).

The richness of Mayan mythology and iconography illuminates their understanding of the cosmos, but what of their understanding of consciousness? Piero Scaruffi argues that "a simple theory of consciousness can be advanced by accepting that the mental is a property of matter." It is an idea that would have resonated with the Classic-era Maya, for whom all matter was an open book in which they could read the spirit world and the true meaning of the universe. For the Maya, consciousness was an active and creative energy, the potential of which can only be realized when people are prepared "to receive the light of knowledge . . . and become beings of eternal luminosity."

14.
THE PROPHECY OF RECOVERED MEMORY

A wave of disgust sweeps through the house of the gods because you forgot life, you forgot your own ancient teaching.

Book of Chilam Balam of Tizimin

The decline of the Maya during the ninth century, the abandonment of their major forest sites and the cultural dislocation produced by the Spanish conquest all contributed greatly to the loss of Mayan teachings. Fortunately, the Maya still had access to a "library" of mythology, genealogy, history and teachings constituted by the hieroglyphic carvings on the walls and stelae of the Mayan temple sites, as well as the four codices that survived the "cultural holocaust" (see pages 53–54). The calendars, based on ancient Mayan formulations of a cyclic concept of time, were also a repository of memory, as was the astronomy on which the calendars were based. The replication of the movements of the stars and planets and the patterns of everyday life combine to form both a record of the past and a glimpse of the future. However, at another level, the true wisdom of the Maya, recorded in their mythology and acted out in rituals by shaman-priests, remained hidden from the Spanish missionaries.

A SERPENT-ENTWINED GOAL set in the vertical walls of Chichén Itzá's great ballcourt. A second type of court, such as the one at Copán, had shallow sloping sides. The ultimate aim of the game was to get the ball through the goal, which was barely larger than the ball itself and therefore difficult to accomplish.

To these memories codified in myth, ritual and art, can be added the kind of intuition referred to in the *Popul Vuh* creation myth, which the gods withheld when creating humans, and knowledge acquired through experience.

THE STORE OF KNOWLEDGE

Native cultures have ways of safeguarding their wisdom. The Maya developed a hieroglyphic alphabet, which they used for their records and a form of book called a codex (see page 58). Some works were almost certainly manuals of complex rituals that arose out of the multilayered Mayan mythology. Every time a ritual was enacted it served as an *aide-mémoire* of different levels of knowledge, thereby ensuring the continuation of a cultural tradition.

The observance of ritual is also a powerful technique for transmitting or teaching wisdom – children watching such rites, and participating when able to do so, are more likely to remember their significance. More importantly, the hieroglyphic carvings on the walls and stelae and throughout the pages of the surviving codices were complemented by a vital oral tradition. The deeper, more esoteric Mayan wisdom would have been committed to memory in the form of mythology, commentaries, poems, songs and discourses, perhaps during the choreography of dances that recounted legends and ancient battles.

As Mayan society became more complex, and the role of individuals and groups became more specialized, the responsibility for memorizing and passing on the ancient wisdom by word of mouth would have been assumed by people dedicated to, and specialized in, the task. Over time this role became associated with particular families, and the privilege of preserving the oral tradition became hereditary. The families of certain modern elders, such as Hunbatz Men and Ajq'ij Roberto Poz Perez, have been custodians of this wisdom for generations, passing it down until the time prescribed by the prophecies when a new generation of teachers would emerge who would return to the ceremonial sites and make the teachings available to the world. Committing traditions to memory was not done around a campfire, but was entrusted to a kind of school, where systematic memorizing of the texts provided "an indispensable complement to the contents of the inscriptions in the monuments and painted books".

Stephen Hawking asked, "Why do we remember the past and not the future?" This prophecy speaks of our recovery of memory in the future – so that we shall know where we have come from, and will have a clear sight of where we are going. The final *baktun*, through which we are now living, is marked as a period of "great forgetting" – it is also the *baktun* in which we shall recover from that amnesia and "echo the memory of the universe".

A GAME ROOTED IN THE ORIGIN MYTHS

A sacred ritual is an acted parable, a drama that can serve as a reminder of some originating mythology. This can even take the form of a ritualized game, and the ballgame (see also page 35) is a striking example of this. The Mayan game re-enacts an account of a creation myth recorded in the *Popul Vuh*.

Two brothers who had been playing the ballgame were called down to the Underworld by the gods, who issued a challenge to test their skills. In fact, it was a trap – the gods had been irritated by the noise and the brothers were decapitated. One head was hung in a tree. A girl approached the tree and the head spat at her. She magically became pregnant and fled to the upper world where she gave birth to twins, Hunahpú and Xbalanqué. When the boys later found their father's ballgame equipment and started to play, the gods summoned them – only this time the gods were to lose.

15.
DESTRUCTION
OF THE EARTH

When Katun 9 Ahau shall arrive later on, then they must all profess my teachings, when that day comes . . . without forsaking them, in the final days of misfortune, in the final days of tying up the bundles of the thirteen katuns on 4 Ahau, then the end of the world shall come and the katun of our fathers will ascend on high.

Book of Chilam Balam of Tizimin

The threat of annihilation was never far from Mayan minds. Since all four of the preceding Sun ages (see page 112) had ended in catastrophe, the Maya were disposed to read the universe in terms of conflict and threat. Ancestral memories of harsh times and natural disasters no doubt helped to shape Mayan culture. Although their civilization had extraordinarily sophisticated aspects, the pessimistic tone of doom and fear were sustained in Mayan rituals throughout the Classic period. However, anyone interpreting this prophecy as a warning that the world will be destroyed at the winter equinox of 2012 is being unduly defeatist. Although the age may end with a disaster, or a series of them, the world will survive.

FLOOD

In Mayan mythology, flooding is associated with both the creation and the destruction of the Earth, and a deluge is

(PREVIOUS PAGES) Many Mesoamerican ballcourts had skull racks (known today by the Aztec word *tzompantli*) where the severed heads of the sacrificed were displayed upon wooden posts. At Chichén Itzá (shown here) there is an inscribed-stone "wall of skulls". The blood that was shed during and after the game was believed to fertilize the earth and help to ensure a bountiful harvest.

one of the most persistent themes in Mayan literature. There was an inundation when the Earth was created, and water seems to be necessary to the restoration of the Earth after its destruction. The regularity with which mention is made of water in the Mayan myths is entirely logical, given that it is so essential to life. The *Dresden Codex* speaks of the destruction of the world by a flood "planned by the Heart of Sky that came down upon the heads of the effigies carved of wood."

Disastrous floods are, of course, a common feature in myths throughout the world, as the biblical story of Noah's flood indicates. Mayan flood imagery also occurs in the *Book of Chilam Balam of Chumayel*: "then in a great sheet of water the waves came. When the great serpent was taken away, the heavens fell and the earth was submerged." Interestingly, the Yucatec word *butic* means both widespread flooding and judgment, a combination that further echoes the Genesis story.

AVERTING DISASTER

The theme of being threatened, and thus the need for foreknowledge – and possible prevention or protection –

THE CAIMAN OF CATASTROPHE

The all-destroying flood is associated in a number of Mayan stories with a huge caiman, sometimes called Itzam Cab Ain ("Giant Fish Earth Caiman"). In some stories the caiman carries the Earth on its back; in others its undulating skin is the Earth's surface; and in one creation account, the entire caiman is the Earth.

Itzam may relate to Itzamná, making the caiman a terrestrial manifestation of the great god. Itzamná was involved in the creation as well as in the re-creation or restoration of the Earth after the various catastrophes that ended each of the five previous world ages, known as Suns.

Diego de Landa recorded in his *Relación de las cosas de Yucatán* a fire-walking ceremony in which a specially prepared caiman represented the flood and the Earth. The saurian's importance in iconography is exemplified by a bench from the palace at Palenque, identified as a cosmological throne decorated with imagery of this Cosmic Monster in the form of a "starry deer alligator" forming an arching element in the heavens.

continues to be a part of the daily rituals of the Maya. Each priest-shaman will have a group of families to safeguard, somewhat like a doctor's medical practice. Neighbouring family lineages have what is called a lineage foundation stone, which at specific times is "opened" by the priest-shaman. During the ritual he itemizes possible natural disasters – notably forest fires, earthquakes and floods – and asks that they do not occur. The ritual, usually performed every nine months (roughly at the end of each *tzolkin* cycle) is a local practice related to the greater cycles, the ends of which portend disaster.

Other than global flooding, causing the Earth to revert to its primal state, what else threatens to destroy the world? The major contenders (see pages 140–147) are threats associated with modifications to the Earth caused by climate change and ecological damage, and the implications of alterations to the Earth's magnetic field.

That this prophecy is interpreted apocalyptically has been criticized by many Mayan elders. Carlos Barrios accuses people of overactive imaginations: "The world will not end. It will be transformed. The indigenous have the calendars, and know how to accurately interpret them, not the others." Despite this more positive outlook, there are many who believe that we could be in for an uneasy passage, and that we might see "chaos and destruction in all the kingdoms of nature."

DESTRUCTION OF A WORLD AGE is believed to be what is depicted in this image from the *Dresden Codex*. A great flood pours from the mouth of a sky serpent, while a goddess appears to add to the catastrophic torrent by emptying the contents of her water jar. At the bottom is another deity, possibly Chac.

16.
EARTH CHANGES:
ECOLOGY AND CLIMATE

The surface of the Earth will be moved. How can the people be protected, thus disturbed in the midst of the Earth, in the sculptured land of the Ichcansiho . . . According to the omens above the Earth and the prophecies, the disturbances of our land shall eventually turn back.

Book of Chilam Balam of Tizimin

This prophecy focuses on one of the most important themes of the Mayan message: our interdependence with nature. The Maya were focused on their relationships with the immediate environment – notably through the weather gods – and with the distant but visible universe. These concerns dominated Mayan mythology and formed the plot behind the dramas of the Maya's rituals.

Changes to our planet have accompanied humans throughout history. It was Darwin's thesis that how well animals adapted was one of the determining factors of their evolution. As the Earth changes so must we, but the process as it affects humans has moved on to include not only physical adaptations, but also attitudes and priorities. Changes in our outlook as well as in our biology may well prove to be indispensable to our survival.

Modern-day summits to highlight ecological deterioration and the multi-faceted challenge of climate change suggest that this prophecy is being fulfilled.

THE LIFE-GIVING WEATHER GODS

The *Popul Vuh* account of creation climaxes with the making of human beings out of maize, emphasizing the importance of this crop to Mayan well-being. The creation account describes how white and yellow corn was ground nine times (representing the nine months of human gestation) and made into a paste by the Bearer Begetter: ". . . they were simply made and modelled . . . the making, the modelling of our first mother-father, with yellow corn, white corn for the flesh, food alone for the human legs and arms, for our first fathers, the four human works."

This myth emphasizes the extent of Mayan dependence on agriculture and the crucial importance of the climatic elements required to bring about any successful harvest. From Mayan astronomical records it is clear that the Maya had some idea of weather patterns and the climatic changes that might take place.

Forest clearance, soil erosion, drought, flood and crop failure may have contributed greatly to the Mayan decline during the ninth century. A *milpa*, or plot of ground cleared of forest, is only viable for two years, which meant that the Maya had to operate a rotation system, leaving used *milpa*s to lie fallow for several years. Once the cut trees had been cleared by fire, the maize seed was planted in holes poked through the ash with a dibble stick. Then the farmer prayed to the gods to bring life-giving rain.

THE RESURRECTED MAIZE GOD

The Maya had several different forms of the maize god. Yum Kaax (see opposite page) is represented with the abundant maize headdress; a foliated maize god with corn sprouting from his head symbolizes growing maize; and there is a tonsured maize god who is the Classic Maya prototype of Hun Hunahpu (of the Quiché Maya's *Popul Vuh*). The latter has an elongated human head that is often shaved in zones across his flattened brow, imitating a ripened ear of corn, with a tuft of hair representing the silk at the tip of the cob. The removal of the ear from the stalk at harvest represents decapitation, the fate of Hun Hunahpu.

The creation mythology in the *Popul Vuh* tells of the Hero Twins searching for their vanquished father, Hun Hunahpu, in the Underworld, with the intention of bringing him back to the surface world; a clear account of the origin of both maize and people, since humans were created from the "resurrected" corn.

This association of maize with resurrection points to the round of the seasons, of human life, of the rising and setting of the sun and of the various cycles represented in the Mayan calendars.

THE MAIZE GOD (left) confronts God K, or Kauil, who has a snout and wears a smoking-axe through his obsidian-mirrored forehead. God K is the deity of lineages and is particularly associated with the ritual of the blood sacrifice.

So indispensable was maize to the Maya that in Yum Kaax it had its own deity, who sometimes manifested as Hun Hunahpu, the father of the Hero Twins. A young, good-looking male god with a headdress of foliated maize, he was evident everywhere – carved onto the doorways and facades of every major temple and on numerous stelae, often in the company of Chac the divinity of rain and lightning. There were also gods of wind, storms, clouds and other forms of weather, all of which stress the Maya's dependence on their climate and their sensitivity to any changes in it. There are echoes of Egyptian civilization's dependence on the levels of the Nile river, and of those gods who they believed helped to control it. The human race is vulnerable to the vicissitudes of the weather, and providing a forecasting, whether by means of astrology or more high-tech modern methods, seems to be a necessity for us – a form of daily divination.

THE MIGHTY RAIN GOD

Water is life, and fresh water is given to us by rain, when "the sky falls down" as the *Popul Vuh* puts it. The rain god Chac is one of Mesoamerica's longest-serving gods, and one of many deities still revered by the Maya today.

Chac is a complicated figure because he is associated with many different mythical and astronomical elements. He is depicted in various ways: for example, he is shown carrying a net and creel, associating him with fishing. Other images give him a long nose, perhaps more human than reptilian, but his body is still scaled and he has a shell-like ear. He is frequently pictured carrying thunderbolt weapons, such as a stone axe in the form of a serpent – itself a representation of lightning – or holding the more obvious symbol of a flaming torch.

In the Palace of the Masks at Kabah in the Yucatán (connected to neighbouring Uxmal by a *sak be*, a Mayan "white road" or ceremonial causeway), there are so many images of Chac that the building is regarded as a shrine dedicated to the rain god. The structure's nickname of *codz-poop* means "a rolled-up mat", which is a derogatory reference to Chac's long, trunk-like nose. Although many are now broken off in part, there are more than 250 huge masks entirely decorating the facades and main structures of the palace, each mask made up of eighteen different blocks of interconnecting stone. To have multiple images of the same god at one place is unusual in Mayan architecture, and it affirms Chac's importance.

As god of the rain so necessary to the growth of maize, it is unsurprising that Chac has a close association with the crop. An ancient myth tells of him striking a rock to release the original maize, a variation of the myth that maize comes from below the earth. Even so, Chac's standing with the Maya is ambivalent and dualistic – he is praised for bringing rain to water the maize, but he is feared for the excess of rain that will destroy it, and for his thunderbolts that might sow destruction. As a benevolent force he brings the weather that ensures the success of the maize crop. As a malevolent power his withdrawal of rain, manifesting in the ensuing drought, brings ruin to the maize and results in famine and misery. Rain is life, drought is death.

It could be said that Chac appears as the god of climate change, affecting health as well as agriculture. In Mayan iconography Chac is linked, as twin Chacs (one for the morning star and one for the evening star), to Venus, which at its most westerly position marks the onset of the rainy season. Chac is also related to the Milky Way, and, as depicted in skyband images, to the Pleiades as well as to the solar year. Over time this god of essential rain has, in fact, evolved into something of an all-inclusive deity.

RESPECT THE PLANET

This prophecy faces modern humankind with outcomes as stark as when Chac withdrew his rain. This time these are not defined by the rainfall but by how we relate to nature.

The prophecy is uncannily prescient of modern ecological concerns. It speaks of the "disturbances of our

THE TEMPLE OF THE WARRIORS is one of two major structures in the main plaza at Chichén Itzá. The other is the pyramid El Castillo. This is the temple entrance, dominated by serpent columns and a sacrificial stone: the recumbent *chacmool*, holding a bowl into which offerings were placed to appease the gods.

land", of the effects of pollution on "the surface of the Earth", and of the spoiling of the Earth's biosphere – the vulnerable crust of our planet's air, land, soils, rock and water, which supports every known form of life. The warning also comes from Carlos Barrios, a contemporary Mayan elder: "Through the ancient techniques of divination and the tools of prophecy, the Mayan elders are calling forth to pay close attention to messages being sent . . . by ongoing Earth-changing events . . . The message is not meant to induce fear, but to give warning of preparation

CENOTE KUKULKAN near Cancún, pierced by rays of sunlight. To the Maya these sinkholes were sacred subterranean realms associated, among other things, with Chac, the rain god. Chac of the east sent rain; of the north sent cold; of the west sent sickness and death; and of the south sent wind.

and the need to remain aware of your surroundings. The elders are concerned about what has been presented in their recent divinations and they call to all humanity to warn their leaders and to work very hard at a spiritual level to prevent the impending destruction."

This "prophecy of Earth changes" is related to Mayan calendric astronomy. It is not just humanity but also our planet that has passed into the final phase of the period of precession – that is, into the great cycle's final twenty-year katun (1992–2012). The Maya understood this to be the "Earth regeneration period" when, as a result of the Earth's conjunction with the sun, the Milky Way and the planets, a new and complete process of purification will begin as part of an age of renewal and re-creation.

CENOTES AND THE DARK, WATERY UNDERWORLD

Cenotes, or sinkholes, are pools of underground water, which in the Yucatán can be large. They are, in effect, underground lakes that have been exposed by the erosion of the covering rock; they may even be connected to underground river systems.

Cenotes provided the Maya with a water supply for everything, from drinking to cooking and cleaning. Where there were none, the Maya built choltunes, bottle-shaped cisterns in which water collected. Without this hydro-technology, human settlement of the region would have been impossible.

The sacred cenote at Chichén Itzá, which means "Mouth of the Well of the Itzas", is dedicated to Chac. Among the many items found in the cenote when it was dredged in the twentieth century were gold bells, rings, masks, figurines, and a large number of bones belonging to men, women and children who had been sacrificed to Chac. Any victim who did not drown after being thrown into the cenote became blessed with the faculties of prophecy and divination.

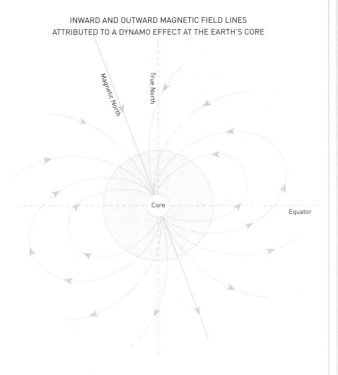

INWARD AND OUTWARD MAGNETIC FIELD LINES
ATTRIBUTED TO A DYNAMO EFFECT AT THE EARTH'S CORE

Magnetic North

True North

Core

Equator

17.
SUNSPOT ACTIVITY AND THE EARTH'S MAGNETIC FIELD

During the . . . tun the heavens will be aflame and the Earth will burn with fire . . . Take care! Whatever happens . . . there will be very high temperatures. . . . Everyone will be dismayed and bitter. . . . There will be fire over men, so that trees . . . will scatter their fruits . . . death will range to and fro in the land.

Book of Chilam Balam of Tizimin

This prophecy speaks of an alteration to the Earth's magnetic field, which is an early indicator of extreme changes in the sun's activity. NASA's projections for 2012 confirm that the intensification of activity in the sun's photosphere, known to science as solar flares, will be extreme enough in 2012 to be felt on Earth. Hunbatz Men has identified various susceptible sites around the world, including Chan Chan in Peru and Mull in Scotland. He suggests that these once sacred places are connected by magnetic fields similar to the ley lines that connect the Mexican pyramids – alignments that shamans believe represent psychic or mystical currents of energy.

The Maya believed that the energy and light of the sun would increase because of the galactic synchronization that will occur on 21 December 2012, at the end of the current precessional cycle. In fact, it is now known that the regions of intense magnetic activity on a star's surface, known as sunspots, have an eleven-year cycle at which point they are maximized because of a reversal of the sun's magnetic field. NASA records show that a "solar maximum" was last reached in 2001.

The 2012 event is predicted to be extreme, perhaps 30–50 percent greater than any geomagnetic storms so far recorded. It will take only a day or two for the Earth's magnetosphere to be disturbed by solar wind shockwaves. Changes in the magnetic field can have minor consequences, such as reversing the direction in which water whirls down a plughole, or more serious ones, such as disturbing the direction-finding senses of dolphins, whales and migrating birds.

Changes to the Earth's magnetic field can also be caused by an impact from a large meteorite or comet, or by an internal event such as a movement of the tectonic plates or of the molten metals in the Earth's core. The Earth experiences regular disruptions known as geomagnetic excursions, and there is a complete reversal of the poles over long periods of time. The process is not well understood. It has happened many times in the past, the last time being nearly 800,000 years ago. A consequence of the reversal is that the Earth's rotation suffers an irregularity which can result in violent winds, earthquakes and volcanic eruptions. Another possible effect is that the Earth will be subjected to damaging cosmic radiation.

A SUN DISC-like eye stares out from a macaw sculpture adorning the ballcourt wall at Copán. In the *Popol Vuh* a vain bird called Seven Macaw believed he was the sun (see page 153), only to be punished for his arrogance by the Hero Twins.

XIBALBA – THE SUNDOWN PLACE OF FRIGHT

Xibalba, the Mayan Underworld, is one of the places where the Maya thought the sun "hid" at night. It was home to a host of wretched creatures – with names such as Scab Stripper, Demon of Pus, Demon of Jaundice and Skull Sceptre – who were shown with gas-distended bellies and wearing necklaces of plucked-out eyeballs.

Commonly thought of as below ground or under water, the entrance to Xibalba might be a cave or a *cenote*. It was also thought to be in the night sky at sundown, visible within the dark part of the Milky Way. The *Popul Vuh* tells us that to arrive in Xibalba was to encounter another world, with its own landscape, rivers, plants and animals.

The ballcourt always included a round marker to represent the entrance to Xibalba. The game itself is a rich symbolic medley that represents the path taken by the sun and replays the mythic struggles of the Hero Twins when they descended to the Underworld to vanquish One Death and Seven Death.

However, a reversal occurred during the period of *Homo erectus* (1.8–1.3 million years ago), which they survived, and there is no evidence of extinctions of other life forms.

THE BRIGHTEST AND BEST

So advanced was the level of astronomy attained by the Maya that it included comprehensive information on solar movements and activity. The Maya plotted eclipses, the position of the sun in relation to the moon and planets, and recorded the cycles of sunspot activity and the effects these had on human life. Solar flare cycles were recorded by the Maya on their Long Count calendar.

This interest in solar activity explains why Kinich Ahau (the "sun-faced lord" or "sun-eyed lord") took centre stage in the pantheon and presided over the Five Suns of the Long Count. There is also an association with the creator god manifested as Kinich Ahau Itzamná.

From the fifth century CE the sun god was identified with kingship. As with the ancient Egyptian pharaohs and the later emperors of the Inca, Mayan rulers expected to be regarded as an incarnation of the sun, and the sun glyph was often part of a king's name. Early iconography used the *kin* glyph for the sun, which also meant "day". However, Kinich Ahau only represented the sun from rising to setting, corresponding to the passage of human life from birth to death. In its underground journey at night the sun manifested as a jaguar (see box, opposite).

The special attributes that were required to occupy a place at the top of the Mayan pantheon form a well-known part of the creation myth in the *Popol Vuh*. Before the sun even existed the vain and arrogant Seven Macaw claimed presumptiously that he could be the sun because he had brilliantly decorated his wings with all kinds of metal ornaments and jewelry, and he wore false teeth of glittering gemstones. He even managed to attract a considerable following among the people of the Earth.

The creator god Huracan asked the Hero Twins to get rid of the impostor. In the struggle that followed, Huracan had his arm torn off by the recalcitrant parrot whose teeth were loosened and whose eye was wounded. The Hero Twins then tried a ruse, posing as an ailing grandparent couple of dentist and doctor. The pair persuaded Seven Macaw to trade Huracan's arm for medical treatment, whereupon they switched his jewelled teeth for white corn and removed all his body ornaments. Deprived of his grandeur and rendered destitute, Seven Macaw's face collapsed and he died.

His two sons were just as arrogant. Zipacna claimed to be the creator of mountains, and Cabrakan, in earthquake mode, their destroyer. Huracan again appealed to the Hero Twins to rid him of the pretenders. The message was that the creator gods wanted important roles to be filled only by candidates with truly exceptional qualities.

FELINE LORD OF THE NIGHT

 The most powerful, feared and respected of all tropical rainforest animals was *balam*, the jaguar. Mainly nocturnal, its luminous eyes shone in the dark like sun discs, explaining the Mayan belief that during its nightly journey the sun was transformed into a supernatural jaguar.

Jaguars had a central role in Mayan religion as well as in that of most other Mesoamerican cultures. They were also important shamanic creatures, and humans in states of transformation had been changing themselves into jaguars from at least Olmec times. *Balam* was part of the title of the jaguar priests who produced works such as the *Book of Chilam Balam of Chumayel*.

In their role as incarnations of the sun, kings dressed in jaguar pelts and wore jewelry fashioned out of jaguar claws and teeth. During some important rituals, jaguars were offered in sacrifice. The pre-eminent totemic animal, the jaguar was a widespread emblem – as well as a popular name – of kings.

Jaguar gods were associated with caves, the night and Xibalba. Sharing the same habitat, the Maya had more jaguar-related gods than other Mesoamerican cultures, among them the Jaguar God of the Underworld, the Water Lily Jaguar and Baby Jaguar.

18.
PROPHECIES
ABOUT EVOLUTION

The great masters, together with the great spirits, will become a unique being, and they will be able to travel as the wind itself, to fall down like the rain does, to heat like the fire does, and, most importantly, to impart sacred knowledge.

Hunbatz Men

The precessional cycle of nearly 26,000 years, which returns us to alignment with the galaxy, is not so much a Mayan prediction or prophecy as an astronomical event that the Maya had plotted in their interconnected calendars. A distinction has to be made between prophecies and actual events; the prophecy is to be found in how the Maya interpreted this phenomenon – that is, how significant they understood its influence to be on human life. The long cycle has been likened to a period of collective gestation that represents our unfolding as a species. From that perspective, this prophecy is about evolution. Darwin argued that adaptation to changes in environment and climate was essential if a species was to ensure its survival – an inability to do so meant probable extinction. The Maya are prophesying that if humanity is to survive in any meaningful way, it will have to continue to adapt, not just physically, but spiritually and mentally, by changing the nature of human consciousness.

LIVES FILLED WITH FEAR

Mayan culture was violent and brutal. Even during the Classic period, fear is evident in Mayan mythology and the iconography that adorns temples and stelae. The Maya feared the Underworld, they feared Venus, they feared the dark rift of the Milky Way, they feared the sunset in case the sun disappeared forever, and they feared the night that followed. They had become accustomed to think in terms of disaster – in the form of plague, war, crop failure, earthquake, drought and flooding.

Given that context, it is remarkable that there were signs of spiritual evolution – changes were taking place within the pantheon of gods, slowly edging the Maya away from polytheism to the worship of Hunab Ku as the one, absolute deity.

In one sense – the nature of their consciousness – it can be argued that the historical Maya were more evolved than we are with our Western outlook. Instead of the nature of their consciousness, it is perhaps better to think in terms of their consciousness of nature. The Maya were

BODY TRANSFORMATION

Most people feel the need to change. At a superficial level this can relate to the way we dress, our hair colour and style, the adornments to our body such as tattoos and jewelry, and so on. At a deeper level the urge to "move on" may change our priorities and spiritual orientation.

The Maya also made much of physical appearance and were known to practise head-shaping and teeth decoration. Flattening of the forehead was popular from around 500BCE. Several varieties of head-shape were achieved by applying sustained pressure to the cranium of an infant. Head-shaping was so widespread that it seems to have had nothing to do with class or social status. There was no medical or therapeutic value – unlike, say, trepanation – though there is some likelihood of there having been a cultural, or even a religious, association. Caimans and snakes appear frequently in Mayan mythology and iconography, and flattening the forehead simulates a reptilian appearance. Could it be that the Maya's wish to reshape themselves was symbolic of a deeper appetite for transformation?

Dental decoration was practised from the age of fifteen. Teeth were filed into points, or ground into rectangles, and drilled with holes so that small pieces of jade, turquoise or polished iron pyrite could be inserted. Many different shapes and patterns were found among the ancient Maya. The ornamentation of teeth seems to have been more popular with women than men.

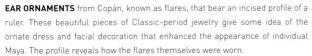

EAR ORNAMENTS from Copán, known as flares, that bear an incised profile of a ruler. These beautiful pieces of Classic-period jewelry give some idea of the ornate dress and facial decoration that enhanced the appearance of individual Maya. The profile reveals how the flares themselves were worn.

a people who lived every moment acutely aware of their environment, of the interdependence of their immediate habitat and the unlimited universe. This was consciousness in a way that is lost to us: they recognized that the patterns of the movements of the sun, moon and planets affected life on Earth, for both the individual and the community. Theirs was a holistic pantheism in the process of evolving into a dynamic cosmology.

It is impossible to say how this might have developed had the Spanish conquest not introduced the influence of Roman Catholic Christianity. However, where the old practices have remained strongest, such as in Guatemala, a seam of vital energy has been formed from a combination of mind, consciousness and spirituality.

Contemporary Mayan shaman-priest Roberto Poz observes: "All spirituality takes time. To know the calendar, and to deepen one's understanding of the calendar, takes time. That is, time to get the threads of one's life straightened and in order. Time to understand the relationships in life. Time to know one's capacities and to deepen one's life. Time to feel the forces of spirituality. After a while, you begin to feel the calendars in your body."

Evolution is not a process that has an end: it will continue as long as there are life-forms on Earth, and for humanity that continued development will be spiritual, affecting the potential of the mind.

THE PALACE OF THE GOVERNOR AT UXMAL

Jaguar throne

Southernmost
rising point of
Venus c.750CE

North

19.
TRANSCENDING
TECHNOLOGY

Katun 2 Ahau is the twelfth katun. For half the katun there will be bread; for half the katun there will be water. It is the word of God. Its bread, water and temple are halved. It is the end of the word of God.

Book of Chilam Balam of Chumayel

This prophecy warns of the "end of the word of God"; that is, the weakening of values that sustain a spiritual perception of life. Katun 2 Ahau, which follows the winter solstice of 2012, will be the first twenty-year period of the new precessional cycle. Previous recurrences of the *katun* have been marked by crises in confidence and ideology, negative developments which have been evident in recent years. Mayan elders today, such as Hunbatz Men and José Argüelles, argue that advanced technology undermines our mental faculties, because machines are carrying out functions once performed by our minds. What is significant is the accelerating rate of technological change, leading to the rise of robotics and artificial intelligence, which have become organic extensions of ourselves. We are in danger of using science and technology to create a society with built-in self-destructive features.

Technologies were developed by the Maya to serve the needs of their society. The Maya were architects, builders and sophisticated agriculturalists, with the skills and tools to produce both high art and the weaponry of war. They had a remarkable knowledge of astronomy and mathematics, which they put to good use to develop their calendars. Little is known of the design and building techniques used for Mayan pyramids, temples and palaces, but construction would inevitably have required intricate planning and posed a formidable management challenge.

MAYAN CREATIVE ARTS

The Maya applied technology with outstanding success to various forms of the creative arts, such as pottery and ceramics, sculpture, wallpaintings, woven textiles and the making of musical instruments. The latter required quite precise scientific knowledge allied to native craft skills, using bone, wood, reeds and ceramics to produce flutes, ocarinas, maracas, horns and various kinds of tympani.

What we know of ancient Mayan arts and crafts is derived from those artefacts made of the most durable materials, such as jade, stone and pottery. Carved wood or painted and woven textiles have not survived. The most precious Mayan material was jade, and it was used to show off the skills of the greatest craftsmen. The lowland Maya also worked with the much rarer marble.

One of the greatest Mayan achievements was the development of an advanced form of hieroglyphic writing,

A PRINCE IN CEREMONIAL DRESS is represented by this painted clay figure, c.800–900ce, holding a rattle and headdress. The piece is actually an ocarina, a flute-like whistle used to provide music for dances and rituals.

THE COSMIC HARMONY OF MAYAN CITIES

The work of the anonymous Mayan architects and master builders represents a variety of regional vernacular styles. Tikal and Chichén Itzá seem entirely functional, while Palenque and Copán are more graceful.

Uxmal, which flourished from 700 to 1000 CE, is open and spacious, and its various levels skilfully use the site's topography to offer views of the green hills, the gleaming limestone outcrops, the red soil and the forest. There is a sense of coordination and balance between the design and ornamentation, its mosaic façades and entablatures displaying sophisticated aesthetic intelligence.

At many of the sites, architects and astronomers would have collaborated to replicate on Earth the patterns of stars visible in the skies above, and many buildings were designed to provide sight lines precisely to locate significant astronomical phenomena. For example, at Uxmal the jaguar throne has been placed in front of the Palace of the Governor so that it is perfectly aligned with the southernmost rising point of Venus (see diagram, page 159).

together with the knowledge of how to produce surfaces on which to record. Lost forever are many bark-paper books, which may have included manuals on building and carving techniques, how to make dyes and paints, or the different ways clay could be worked for pottery and ceramics. A range of techniques existed to make, inscribe and decorate pottery, the ceramic surfaces of which became canvases for scenes of courtly life, the Underworld, portraits of the gods, and episodes from mythology.

Rather than being worked on a potter's wheel, vessels were formed from coiled lengths of clay, or built up using thin slabs of clay. The walls of these were then smoothed out and shaped by hand. The finished items were set aside to dry, and then painted. Finally, the pots were fired in kilns that burned wood or charcoal. Brilliant chromatic effects were achieved by firing the pots at low temperatures, because aesthetics were more important than durability.

The technologies the Maya used to build, to make practical artefacts, and to hone their arts and crafts skills were entirely integrated into their culture, and wholly expressive of it. Everything they created, it seems, contributed to the quality of their lives. By transmitting this prophecy, the Mayan elders are telling us that our technology has gone beyond the point of securing a better quality of life. Our culture is defined by its productivity, and consequently by people's acquisitiveness and materialistic values. We are warned that we must transcend our technology before it transcends us.

20.
THE PROPHECY
OF TIME

*A time will come when the **katun**-folds will have passed away, when they will be found no longer, because the count of **tuns** is reunited.*

Book of Chilam Balam of Tizimin

This prophecy is about the nature of time and how to perceive it, taking us to the heart of the Mayan message that time is cyclic and not linear. Living through the last *katun* of this precessional cycle, we are well placed to appreciate that each time the cycle turns we have the opportunity to make our lives better. Time is, of course, related to space and that the Maya understood this interrelationship is proved by their calendars. The Western mind tends toward dualism, setting ideas in opposition rather than in harmony. For example, to regard space and time as different entities is reflective of a culture that wants to make distinctions. Our minds separated spirit and matter, mind and matter, and – until Einstein and the new physics – space and time.

The Maya believed that the proper context for the very brief period of time a human is alive is the lengthy period during which the celestial bodies of our galaxy move in predictable patterns. These changes of the cosmos were measured and recorded by Maya astronomers, whose wisdom led them to conclude that human life should be synchronized with the changes. They realized that linear time was a construct of the mind, a tool that enabled life to be organized or the length of a king's reign to be measured. Our consciousness of linear time is like a tiny, seemingly straight part of the circumference of time's greater curve – that is to say, where we find ourselves, between birth and death, on the wheel of time.

In whatever way we are conscious of time, we are not all conscious of the *same* time. The Maya understood this, which is why they had different systems of timekeeping for biological, astrological, religious and social realities. These various aspects of time overlapped in the same way as the intermeshing cycles of their calendars.

THE *CODEX TROANA CORTESIANUS*, better known as the *Madrid Codex*, is composed entirely of almanacs organized in terms of the 260-day ritual calendar used throughout Mesoamerica for divination and prophecy.

THIRTEEN-MOON "NATURAL TIME" CALENDAR

Dr José Argüelles, a Mexican-American scholar who has assumed the name Valum Votan and the epithet Messenger of the Law of Time, advocates a calendar based on thirteen cycles of the moon. He argues it would reflect "natural time" by providing a system rooted in order, perfection and simplicity; one that would permit the harmonic convergence of humanity.

In this view, the Gregorian calendar, and the measurement of time by clocks and watches, are artificial. For many cultures around the world, time is measured by their agriculture, by seasonal changes and by their own life-cycles. Time is a sensual perception rather than a system of notation.

The thirteen-moon calendar is the simplest way to reprogram our daily awareness of the actual nature of time because for every one time that we go around the sun, the moon goes around the Earth thirteen times. The year has already been divided by nature.

Argüelles calls the system Dreamspell, and he believes that this method of time-keeping would bring ancient Mayan time-science to our own culture. However, this calendar is not Mayan, and it has no relationship with the *haab* and *tzolkin* that make the Calendar Round, for which reason it is not compatible with dates and methods used by the Maya in Guatemala today. However, the alternative calendar is valid on its own terms. Adopting it might be one way the prophecy could be fulfilled – namely that we adjust to a cyclic view of time based on the interconnected movements of the Earth, moon and sun.

21.
THE PROPHECY THAT WE ARE THE PROPHECY

In their own time, the Maya saw their prophecy about the coming of strangers and a new religion fulfilled. The prophecy about the rediscovery of the old ceremonial sites, and the return of the Maya to the pyramids and temples abandoned toward the end of the Classic period, has been fulfilled in part. That of the emergence of a new generation of teachers, drawn from people throughout the cultures and races of the world, is also in the process of being fulfilled. The recurring themes of all the other prophecies point to the many problems of ecology and climate, to the dangers of materialism and hyper-technology, to the need for the human race to overcome its differences, to the necessary recovery of wisdom, and to the nature of consciousness. All the prophecies are focused on the period of time around the winter equinox of 2012, when the Long Count calendar terminates and the current precessional cycle ends. Because we are living during this period, the prophecies are about us.

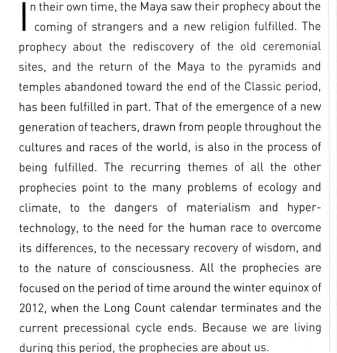

This is the record of the wisdom of the book in which is set down the course of each katun . . . whether it is good or bad. These things shall be accomplished. No one shall cause them to cease.

Book of Chilam Balam of Chumayel

THE GIVING OF THE PROPHECIES

Mayan culture developed a distinctive combination of concepts relating to time and prophecy. This distinctiveness was the product of Mayan mythological beliefs, the Mayan prophetic tradition, the Maya's remarkable knowledge of astronomy and mathematics, their dedicated cult of shaman-priests, and their means of receiving and transmitting the prophecies.

The *chilam balam* of Tizimin, the author of one of the surviving manuscripts, described how prophecies were given. His account is thought to be typical of the methods used by these seers: "He went into a room in his home and lay down, passing into a trance-like state. The communicating god or spirit sat on the ridge of the house and spoke to the unconscious *chilam*. When it was finished, other priests gathered in what may have been the reception hall of the house and listened as the receiving prophet told his message. They kept their faces to the floor."

What might be called "true" prophecy is not dependent on the skills of the shaman-priest, or the way in which a prophecy is delivered: it lies solely in the contribution one makes to the already received tradition. A relationship can be made between prophecy and evolution, since the message, or meaning, of the prophecy is a development or advancement of an idea. The value and authenticity of prophecy can only be measured by the extent to which it matures the spirituality of those receiving it.

THE AGE OF RESPONSIBILITY

This prophecy is about responsibility. No one can choose when they live and it is by chance that we are living in what the Greeks called *kairos*, "the right moment". As Carl Jung observed: ". . . Coming generations will have to take account of this momentous transformation if humanity is not to destroy itself through the might of its own technology and

THE TEMPLE OF THE WARRIORS at Chichén Itzá in Yucatán. In front of the temple are dozens of columns, each carved with militaristic reliefs, which form part of a once-roofed structure known as the Mansion of the Warriors. Built at the height of Chichén Itzá's power, within centuries the city had been conquered.

science. . . . So much is at stake and so much depends on the psychological constitution of the modern man."

The philosopher Karl Jaspers coined the phrase "axial age" to define the period 800–200BCE, during which dynamic, revolutionary thinking occurred simultaneously in China, India, ancient Greece and the Near East. In that period the world was given philosophies and concepts that have determined its cultures, laws and beliefs ever since – from Confucius, Laozi, the authors of the Upanishads, Siddhartha Gautama, the Old Testament prophets, Homer, Plato and Socrates among others. Later periods can also be considered axial, such as the Renaissance, the Reformation, the Age of Enlightenment and the past century when science and technology have changed the

world radically. The Mayan middle and late Pre-Classic period falls within Jaspers' original axial age, and what the Maya achieved in mathematics and astronomy, calendric astrology and prophecy, could be said to have been developed by them with the world of the early twenty-first century in mind.

Except for those few that spoke to the Maya's own history, the prophecies were not given for themselves but were intended to be transmitted and made available to the world during the *katun*s leading to 21 December 2012. What can we expect as the precession of the equinoxes draws nearer? The fact is, we do not know what will happen. Despite the dangers and problems set out in the prophecies, it is now a matter of how people respond. That we are the prophecy makes us the agents for the radical changes that must be made, but the message is positive and optimistic: "These things shall be accomplished. No one shall cause them to cease."

FURTHER READING

Christenson, Allen. (Translator.) *Popul Vuh: The Sacred Book of the Maya.* Austin: University of Texas Press, 1995.

Coe, Michael, D. *Breaking the Mayan Code.* London: Penguin Books, 1994.

Coe, Michael D. *The Maya.* (6th edition.) London and New York: Thames and Hudson, 1999.

Grube, Nikolai. (Editor.) *Maya: Divine Kings of the Rain Forest.* Cologne: Konemann, 2000.

Houston, S.D. *Maya Glyphs.* London: British Museum Press, 1989.

Laughton, Timothy. *The Maya: Life, Myth and Art.* London: Duncan Baird Publishers, 1998.

Longhena, Maria. *Maya Script: A Civilization and its Writing.* New York and London: Abbeville Press, 2006.

Makemson, Maud W. *The Book of the Jaguar Priest, a Translation of the Book of Chilam Balam of Tizimin with Commentary.* New York: Henry Schuman, Inc., 1951.

Milbrath, Susan. *Star Gods of the Maya: Astronomy in Art, Folklore, and Calendars.* Austin: University of Texas Press, 1999.

Miller, M. and Taube, K. *An Illustrated Dictionary of the Gods and Symbols of Ancient Mexico and the Maya.* London: Thames and Hudson, 1997.

Roys, Ralph L. (Translator.) *The Book of Chilam Balam of Chumayel.* Norman: University of Oklahoma Press, 1967.

Schele, Linda and Freidel, David. *A Forest of Kings: The Untold Story of the Ancient Maya.* New York: William Morrow, 1990.

Schele, Linda., Freidel, David., and Parker, Joy. *Maya Cosmos: Three Thousand Years On the Shaman's Path.* New York: William Morrow, 1993.

Schele, Linda and Mathews, Peter. *The Code of Kings.* New York: Simon and Schuster, 1998.

Schele, Linda and Miller, Mary Ellen. *The Blood of Kings: Dynasty and Ritual in Maya Art.* Forth Worth: Kimbell Art Museum, 1986.

Stierlin, Henri. *The Maya: Palaces and Pyramids of the Rainforest.* Cologne and London: Taschen, 1997.

Taube, Karl. *Aztec and Maya Myths.* London: British Museum Press, 1993.

TEXT REFERENCES

PROPHECY 1 Coe, Michael D. *The Maya* (1999). **Haug, G.H., Gunter, D., Peteson, L.C., Sigman, D.M., Hughen, K.A., and Aeschlimann, B.** "Climate and the Collapse of Maya Civilization" in *Science*, Vol.299, No.5613, 14 March 2003, pp.1731–1735. **Makemson, Maud W.** *The Book of the Jaguar Priest* (1951). **Roys, Ralph L.** *The Book of Chilam Balam of Chumayel* (1967).

PROPHECY 2 Eliade, Mircea. *Shamanism: Archaic Techniques of Ecstasy.* Princeton, New Jersey: Princeton University Press, 2004. **Men, Hunbatz.** *Secrets of Mayan Science/Religion.* Rochester, Vermont: Bear & Company Publishing, 1990. **Roys, Ralph L.** *The Book of Chilam Balam of Chumayel* (1967). **Yaxk'in, Aluna Joy.** "Mayan Prophesy: the Reawakening of the Cosmic Human". See www.v-j-enterprises.com/mayanpr.html

PROPHECY 3 Coe, Michael D. *The Maya* (1999). **Housden, Roger.** *Sacred Journeys in a Modern World.* London: Simon and Schuster, 1998. **Makemson, Maud W.** *The Book of the Jaguar Priest* (1951). **Men, Hunbatz.** "Mayan Prophecies for the New Millennium". See www.13moon.com

PROPHECY 4 Men, Hunbatz. *Secrets of Mayan Science/Religion* (1990). **Roys, Ralph L.** *The Book of Chilam Balam of Chumayel* (1967). **Miller, M. and Taube, K.** *An Illustrated Dictionary of the Gods and Symbols of Ancient Mexico and the Maya* (1997). **Schele, Linda and Freidel, David.** *A Forest of Kings* (1990). **Tozzer, Alfred, M.** *A Comparative Study of the Mayas and the Lacandones.* Archaeological Institute of America, 1907.

PROPHECY 5 Jenkins, John Major. *Maya Cosmogenesis 2012.* Rochester, Vermont: Bear & Company Publishing, 1998. **Matthews, Peter.** "Who's Who in the Classic Maya World" at Foundation for the Advancement of Mesoamerican Studies, www.famsi.org; Pacal Votan at www.13moon.com and www.lawoftime.org. **Robertson, Merle Green.** *Sculpture of Palenque. Volume 1: The Temple of Inscriptions.* Princeton, New Jersey: Princeton University Press, 1983. **Schele, Linda and Freidel, David.** *A Forest of Kings* (1990).

PROPHECY 6 Christenson, Allen. *Popul Vuh* (1995). **Davis, Joel.** *Journey to the Centre of our Galaxy.* Chicago: Contemporary Books, 1991. **Jenkins, John Major.** *Maya Cosmogenesis 2012.* Rochester, Vermont: Bear & Company Publishing, 1998. **Roys, Ralph L.** "The prophecies for the Maya tuns or years in the Books of Chilam Balam of Tizimin and Mani" in *Contributions to American Anthropology and History*, 10 (51): pp.153–186. Carnegie Institution of Washington, Washington DC, 1949.

PROPHECY 7 Longhena, Maria. *Maya Script* (2006). **Roys, Ralph L.** *The Book of Chilam Balam of Chumayel* (1967). **Tedlock, Dennis. (Translator.)** *Popul Vuh.* New York: Touchstone, 1996.

TEXT REFERENCES

PROPHECY 8 Argüelles, José. *Time and the Technosphere: The Law of Time in Human Affairs*. Rochester, Vermont: Bear & Company Publishing, 2002. Coe, Michael D. *The Maya* (1999). Longhena, Maria. *Maya Script* (2006). Makemson, Maud W. *The Book of the Jaguar Priest* (1951). Miller, M. and Taube, K. *An Illustrated Dictionary of the Gods and Symbols of Ancient Mexico and the Maya* (1997). Roys, Ralph L. *The Book of Chilam Balam of Chumayel* (1967).

PROPHECY 9 Bonewitz, Ronald. *Maya Prophecy*. London: Judy Piatkus Ltd., 1999. Calleman, Carl Johan. *The Mayan Calendar and the Transformation of Consciousness*. Rochester, Vermont: Bear & Company Publishing, 2004. Christenson, Allen. *Popul Vuh* (1995). Jenkins, John Major. *Maya Cosmogenesis 2012*. Rochester, Vermont: Bear & Company Publishing, 1998. Longhena, Maria. *Maya Script* (2006). Martineau, John. *A Little Book of Coincidence in the Solar System*. Glastonbury: Wooden Books Ltd, 2006. Miller, M. and Taube, K. *An Illustrated Dictionary of the Gods and Symbols of Ancient Mexico and the Maya* (1997)

PROPHECY 10 Gilbert, Adrian G. and Cotterell, Maurice M. *The Mayan Prophecies*. Element, 1995. Roys, Ralph L. *The Book of Chilam Balam of Chumayel* (1967). Barrios, Carlos. *The Book of Destiny*. London: HarperCollins, 2009.

PROPHECY 11 Havel, Vaclav. "The Spiritual Roots of Democracy", an address given to the Law School of Stanford University, September 1994. Makemson, Maud W. *The Book of the Jaguar Priest* (1951). Pacal Votan at www.13moon.com and www.lawoftime.org. Roys, Ralph L. *The Book of Chilam Balam of Chumayel* (1967).

PROPHECY 12 From Yabun Chan, cited in Makemson, Maud W. *The Book of the Jaguar Priest* (1951). Miller, M. and Taube, K. *An Illustrated Dictionary of the Gods and Symbols of Ancient Mexico and the Maya* (1997). Longhena, Maria. *Maya Script* (2006).

PROPHECY 13 Jenkins, John Major. *Maya Cosmogenesis 2012*. Rochester, Vermont: Bear & Company Publishing, 1998. Men, Hunbatz. *The Sacred Manuscript of K'altun*. Mérida, Mexico: Mayan Initiation Centres, undated. Milbrath, Susan. *Star Gods of the Maya* (1999). Scaruffi, Piero. *The Nature of Consciousness*. Omniware, 2006.

PROPHECY 14 Gilbert, Adrian. *The End of Time. The Mayan Prophecies Revisited*. Edinburgh: Mainstream Publishing, 2006. Hawking, Stephen. *A Brief History of Time*. London: Guild Publishing, 1990. Makemson, Maud W. *The Book of the Jaguar Priest* (1951). Léon-Portilla, Miguel. (Editor.) *Native Mesoamerican Spirituality*. London: SPCK, 1980.

PROPHECY 15 Calleman, Carl Johan. *The Mayan Calendar and the Transformation of Consciousness* (2004). Christenson, Allen. *Popul Vuh* (1995). Longhena, Maria. *Maya Script* (2006). Makemson, Maud W. *The Book of the Jaguar Priest* (1951). Roys, Ralph L. *The Book of Chilam Balam of Chumayel* (1967). Taube, Karl A. "Caimans, Cosmology, and Calendrics in Postclassic Yucatan". *Research Reports on Ancient Maya Writing 26*. Washington, D.C.: Center for Maya Research, 1989. Taube, Karl A. *Aztec and Maya Myths* (1998). Tedlock, Barbara. *Time and the Highland Maya*. University of New Mexico Press, 1992.

PROPHECY 16 Coe, Michael D. *The Maya* (1999). Makemson, Maud W. *The Book of the Jaguar Priest* (1951). Milbrath, Susan. *Star Gods of the Maya* (1999). Tedlock, Dennis. *Popul Vuh* (1996). Miller, M. and Taube, K. *An Illustrated Dictionary of The Gods and Symbols of Ancient Mexico and the Maya* (1997). Taube, Karl A. *Aztec and Maya Myths* (1998).

PROPHECY 17 Longhena, Maria. *Maya Script* (2006). Men, Hunbatz. "Mayan Prophecies for the New Millennium" – see www.13moon.com. Miller, M. and Taube, K. *An Illustrated Dictionary of The Gods and Symbols of Ancient Mexico and the Maya* (1997).

PROPHECY 18 Jenkins, John Major. *Maya Cosmogenesis 2012* (1998). Men, Hunbatz. "Initiation in the Mayan Consciousness" at the Prophets' Conference, Victoria, Canada 2001. Molesky-Poz, Jean. *Contemporary Maya Spirituality*. Austin: University of Texas Press, 2006. Tiesler, Vera. "Head Shaping and Dental Decoration Among the Ancient Maya", a paper presented to the 64th Meeting of the Society of American Archaeology, Chicago, 1999.

PROPHECY 19 Birch, Charles. *A Purpose for Everything: Religion in Postmodern Word View*. Mystic, Connecticut: Twenty-third Publications, 1990. Coe, Michael D. *The Maya* (1999). Drew, David. *The Lost Chronicles of the Maya Kings*. Berkeley: University of California Press, 1999. Roys, Ralph L. *The Book of Chilam Balam of Chumayel* (1967).

PROPHECY 20 Argüelles, José. *Time and the Technosphere*. Rochester, Vermont: Bear & Company Publishing, 2002. See www.lawoftime.org. Makemson, Maud W. *The Book of the Jaguar Priest* (1951). Tedlock, Barbara. *Time and the Highland Maya*. Albuquerque: University of New Mexico Press, 1982.

PROPHECY 21 Jung, C.G. *The Undiscovered Self*. London: Routledge, 1990. Makemson, Maud W. *The Book of the Jaguar Priest* (1951). Roys, Ralph L. *The Book of Chilam Balam of Chumayel* (1967).

IMAGE REFERENCES

ARTWORK CAPTIONS

PROPHECY 1, page 48 the foliated cross, a traditional Mayan symbol seen at Palenque; **PROPHECY 2**, page 56 Hunab Ku symbol; **PROPHECY 3**, page 62 Mayan pyramid temple rising out of the jungle; **PROPHECY 4**, page 68 Kulkukan; **PROPHECY 5**, page 76 Pacal Votan; **PROPHECY 6**, page 84 stylized masks from a palace frieze representing the sun, moon and Saturn; **PROPHECY 7**, page 88 a ceiba tree emerging from the body of Pacal Votan; **PROPHECY 8**, page 96 the Mayan moon goddess Ixchel; **PROPHECY 9**, page 102 Lahun Chan, malign deity; **PROPHECY 10**, page 110 Mayan constellation of the bat (Aquarius), suspended from a skyband; **PROPHECY 11**, page 118 Mayan costumes which reflect social class differences; **PROPHECY 12**, page 122 Kinich Ahau, the sun god; **PROPHECY 13**, page 126 Chac, god of lighting, rain and thunder; **PROPHECY 14**, page 130 a Mayan scribe; **PROPHECY 15**, page 134 the "flood caiman"; **PROPHECY 16**, page 140 head of Chac; **PROPHECY 17**, page 148 jaguar patterned with the *kin* glyph for the sun; **PROPHECY 18**, page 154 Mayan figure achieving realization; **PROPHECY 19**, page 158 the maize god Hun Hunahpu resurrected from the earth, represented by a turtle shell; **PROPHECY 20**, page 162 the Mayan conception of the fourfold nature of universe and of the 260-day ritual calendar; **PROPHECY 21**, page 166 abstract pattern of two ceiba trees making an Earth shape.

GLYPH IDENTIFICATION

Introduction, page 14 "to come from", page 30 "Palenque", page 32 "Itzamná", page 35 "ball-playing youth", page 38 (clockwise from the top), "north" "east", "south", "west", page 41 "Ik", page 43 "Copán", page 46 "Hunab Ku"; **PROPHECY 1**, page 53 "book" or "paper"; **PROPHECY 2**, page 58 "writing"; **PROPHECY 3**, page 64 "Tikal"; **PROPHECY 4**, page 70 "Kukulcan" (both), page 73 "Chichen Itza"; **PROPHECY 5**, page 79 "stone", page 80 "Yum Kaax"; **PROPHECY 6**, page 86 "to count"; **PROPHECY 7**, page 92 "it will happen"; **PROPHECY 8**, page 98 "eclipse"; **PROPHECY 11**, page 120 "to die"; **PROPHECY 12**, page 125 "Kinich"; **PROPHECY 13**, page 128 "alligator"; **PROPHECY 14**, page 133 "ballcourt"; **PROPHECY 15**, page 138 "water"; **PROPHECY 16**, page 142 "corn", page 147 "Chac"; **PROPHECY 17**, page 150 "cave", page 153 "jaguar"; **PROPHECY 18**, page 156 "earspool" or "[ear] flare"; **PROPHECY 19**, page 161 "pyramid"; **PROPHECY 20**, page 164 "moon-length 29 days".

INDEX

Page numbers in *italics* refer to captions